W9-BIW-562

Scott The Piano Guy's™
Favorite Piano Fake Book

ISBN-13: 978-1-4234-1317-2
ISBN-10: 1-4234-1317-2

HAL•LEONARD®
CORPORATION
7777 W. BLUEMOUND RD. P.O. BOX 13819 MILWAUKEE, WI 53213

For all works contained herein:
Unauthorized copying, arranging, adapting, recording or public performance is an infringement of copyright.
Infringers are liable under the law.

Visit Hal Leonard Online at
www.halleonard.com

Contents

Some notes from Scott...

I hope you're as thrilled with this fake book as I have been creating it! Through the feedback from thousands of television show viewers, many of whom were just starting down the path of non-classical piano playing, I was able to include all the things that everyone most wanted and needed in a fake book. I'm proud to say that I listened! It's all in this first-of-its-kind fake book.

Having said that, I need to explain a few things that I think will answer many of the questions you may have when you dig into playing your favorite tunes.

How to Use the Chord Charts

You'll immediately notice that at the beginning of every tune, there is a set of chord diagrams split into an upper and lower row. The upper row contains diagrams of the basic chords designated by the symbols used in the tune. Immediately below every basic chord is a possible chord substitution that you may want to try and use as you begin to get the tune "under hand." These more advanced chords are simply substitutions that professional players tend to use when they are really out working gigs. You will find that they will sound a little more polished, or perhaps jazzy (for lack of a better description). Understand that these more advanced substitutions are not cast in stone. There is no absolute right or wrong choice when choosing whether or not to play the basic or the more advanced chords. Let your ear and taste be your guide. Also, there will be times when the basic and advanced chords listed are exactly the same. That usually occurs where there is just no logical chord substitution to be made.

I think the chord diagrams are the best part of my fake book, because they will allow you to kind of "get into a real player's head" a bit and start to understand why even if you play basic chords perfectly as listed in a lead sheet, you still might not sound like players that you hear out working professionally. Professionals tend to use more hip-sounding chord substitutions for the basic chord symbols given in a lead sheet. Now you can start to get a handle on some of those substitutions. You'll find that similar chord substitutions occur over and over, which will allow you to start internalizing and allowing them to sneak into your playing very naturally.

One Substitute to Watch Out For!

I think you'll quickly notice that one chord substitution is made time and time again: using a major 7th chord instead of a regular old major chord (i.e. C becomes Cmaj7). It is a great substitution that sounds great most of the time but has one major issue to watch out for: If the melody note that is being emphasized when you play the chord happens to be the root of the chord, you probably shouldn't use the substitution. For example:

You have a C chord symbol given above a melody line that has E,F,G in that measure. Great! Go ahead and use the major 7th substitution and play a Cmaj7 instead of the regular C chord.

However, if you have a C chord symbol given above a melody line that has a single C note held through the measure—watch out! Because the C in the melody line is the root of the C chord, it will tend to clash if you use the Cmaj7 as a substitute.

To give your ear a chance to hear this, just play any major 7th chord with your left hand while emphasizing the root note (the note the chord begins with) in your right hand in some octave above where you are playing the chord. It's pretty dissonant... So to be safe, just keep a look out for that "major 7th for a major" chord substitution when the melody line happens to be focusing on the root of the chord. You'll probably be happier just sticking to the original chord.

Voicings

Voicings is a term used for different variations of a chord that you can play that don't necessarily contain every note in the chord. Voicings give you the parts of a chord to leave out to make them simpler to play and still sound great. In most cases in the chord diagrams in this book, we have given you the entire chord in root position. It will be up to you to decide on using a voicing or not, depending on your taste and skill level. However, in a few cases (primarily 13th chords) we went ahead and gave you the chord diagram using a voicing when there was one very obvious one to use. Let me explain further...

You may have noticed that in the case of 9th chords, there are 5 notes. Playing all 5 of those notes is not only very difficult physically to finger, but can also sound a little "muddy." In the real world, players would seldom play all five notes in the 9th chord. Instead they would use a voicing to give them a simpler, cleaner-sounding version of the chord to play. For example, instead of playing all 5 notes in a C9 chord, which are C, E, G, B-flat, D, I would probably choose to play just the E, B-flat, D in the chord (and maybe try to reach down and play the C root separately an octave lower).

This topic is more advanced than can be dealt with here in any depth, so I encourage you to find a book that deals with voicings to learn more. One tip I can give you is that the most important notes in a chord to play (which you need to know to be able to decide which ones to leave out) are the 3rd, 7th, and whatever else is in there that gives the chord its distinctive sound, like the 9th or 13th.

Slash Chords
(D/C, Fmaj7/G, Dm/E for example)

In lead sheet notation, slash chords direct you to play a particular note in the bass (in other words the lowest note you hear). They work like this:

- Whatever the chord symbol is to the left of the slash is the actual chord you are supposed to play.

- Whatever the individual note name is to the right of the slash is the single note you are supposed to play in the bass.

For example, G/A means play a single A note down low in the bass (grab it with your sustain pedal to keep it sounding), and come up and play a G major chord in its normal position. In other words, play a G major chord over an A in the bass.

Am/C means play an A minor chord over a C in the bass. In this case the C is actually a note in the A minor chord. So another way you could look at it is that it is forcing you to play the A minor chord in an inversion with C on the bottom.

Know that sometimes the bass note is in the chord; sometimes it is not. You still just make sure that it is the lowest note you are playing.

For the slash chord in the chord diagrams of this fake book, we are showing you only the chord portion of the slash chord, not the bass note portion. Therefore it is your responsibility to get that bass note played even though it does not appear in the chord diagram.

Have fun! Scott

AMAZING GRACE

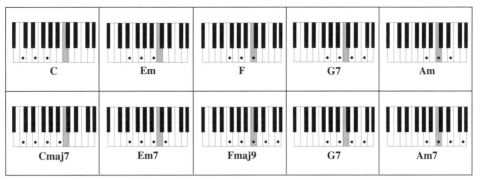

Copyright © 2002 by HAL LEONARD CORPORATION
International Copyright Secured   All Rights Reserved

Words by JOHN NEWTON
From A Collection of Sacred Ballads
Traditional American Melody
From Carrell and Clayton's Virginia Harmony
Arranged by Edwin O. Excell

ALL THE THINGS YOU ARE

from VERY WARM FOR MAY

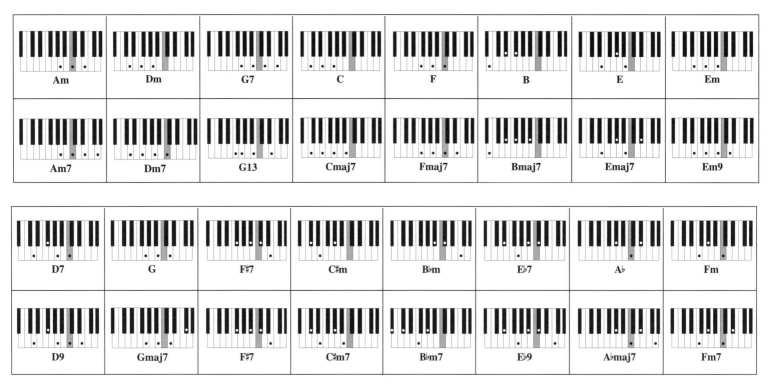

Copyright © 1939 UNIVERSAL - POLYGRAM INTERNATIONAL PUBLISHING, INC.
Copyright Renewed
All Rights Reserved   Used by Permission

Lyrics by OSCAR HAMMERSTEIN II
Music by JEROME KERN

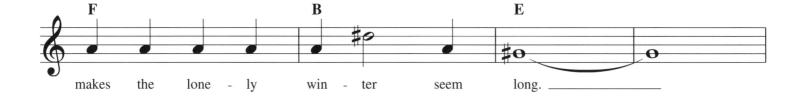

You are the prom-ised kiss of spring-time that

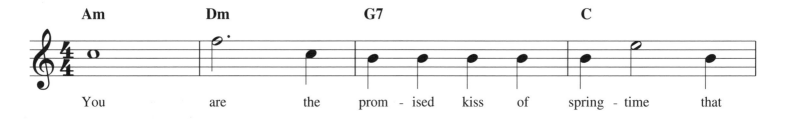

makes the lone-ly win-ter seem long. _____

You are the breath-less hush of eve-ning that

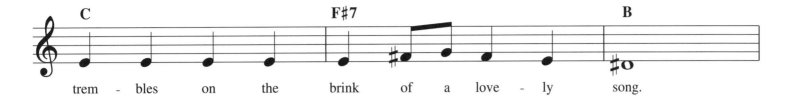

trem - bles on the brink of a love - ly song.

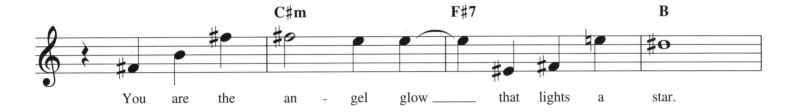

You are the an - gel glow _____ that lights a star.

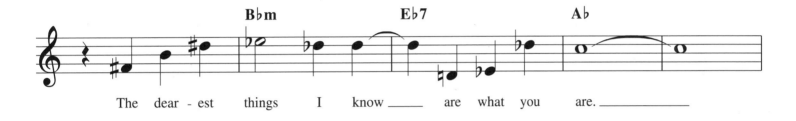

The dear - est things I know _____ are what you are. _____

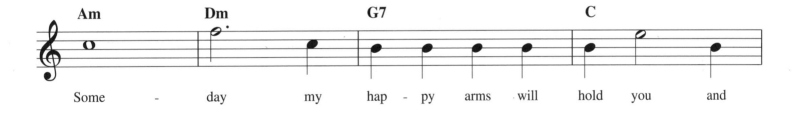

Some - day my hap - py arms will hold you and

some - day I'll know that mo - ment di -

vine, when all the things you are are mine.

AUTUMN LEAVES

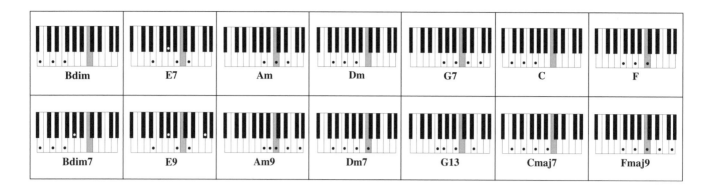

© 1947, 1950 (Renewed) ENOCH ET CIE
Sole Selling Agent for U.S. and Canada:
    MORLEY MUSIC CO., by agreement with ENOCH ET CIE
All Rights Reserved

English lyric by JOHNNY MERCER
French lyric by JACQUES PREVERT
Music by JOSEPH KOSMA

The fall-ing

leaves___ drift by my win-dow, ___ the au-tumn leaves ___ of red and gold. I see your

lips,___ the sum-mer kiss-es, ___ the sun-burned hands ___ I used to hold. Since you

went a-way___ the days grow long,___ and soon I'll hear ___ old win-ter's song. But I

miss you most of all my dar-ling, when au-tumn leaves start to fall.

BLUE SUEDE SHOES
from G.I. BLUES

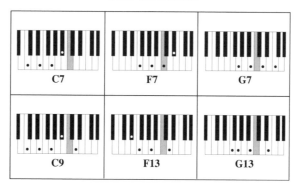

© 1955, 1956 HI-LO MUSIC, INC.
© Renewed 1983, 1984 CARL PERKINS MUSIC, INC. (Administered by WREN MUSIC CO.,
   A Division of MPL Music Publishing, Inc.)
All Rights Reserved

Words and Music by
CARL LEE PERKINS

C7

Well it's one for the mon-ey, two for the show, three to get read-y now

F7   **C7**

go, cat, go but don't you step on my blue suede shoes.

G7   **C7**

You can do an-y-thing_ but lay off of my blue suede shoes._____

Well you can knock me down,_ step on my face,_ slan-der my name all

o-ver the place._ Do an-y-thing that you want to do but uh-uh hon-ey, lay

F7   **C7**

off of my shoes._ Don't you step on my blue suede shoes._____

BLUEBERRY HILL

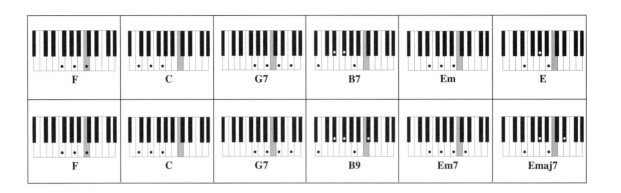

Copyright © 1940 by Chappell & Co.
Copyright Renewed, Assigned to Chappell & Co., Larry Stock Music Co. and Sovereign Music Corp.
All Rights for Larry Stock Music Co. Administered by Larry Spier, Inc., New York
International Copyright Secured   All Rights Reserved

Words and Music by AL LEWIS,
LARRY STOCK and VINCENT ROSE

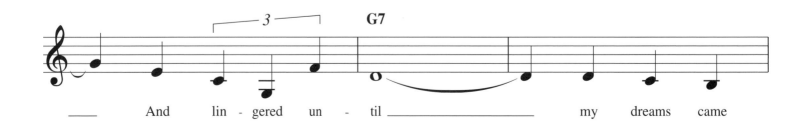

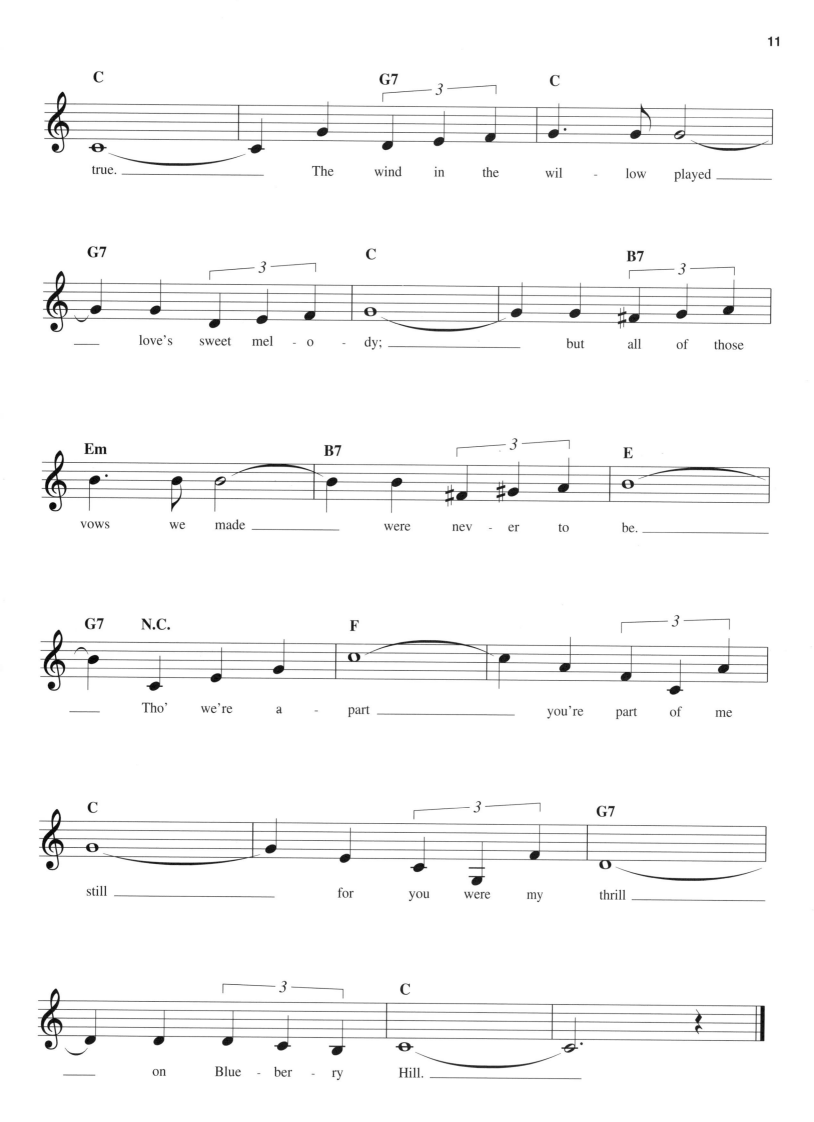

BYE BYE BLACKBIRD
from PETE KELLY'S BLUES

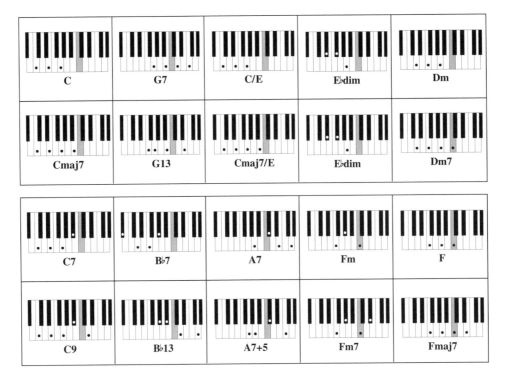

Copyright © 1926 (Renewed 1953)
All rights for the extended term administered by Fred Ahlert Music Corporation on behalf of Olde Clover Leaf Music
All rights for the extended term administered by Ray Henderson Music on behalf of Ray Henderson
International Copyright Secured   All Rights Reserved

Lyric by MORT DIXON
Music by RAY HENDERSON

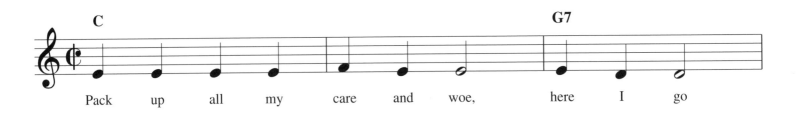

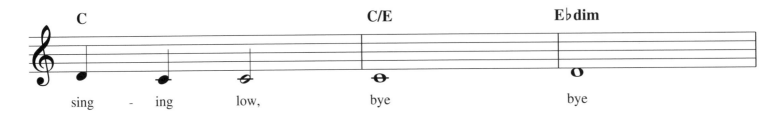

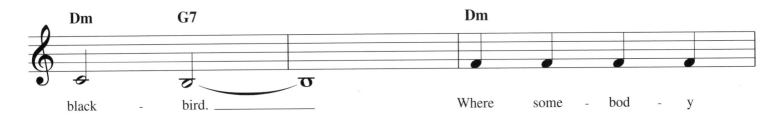

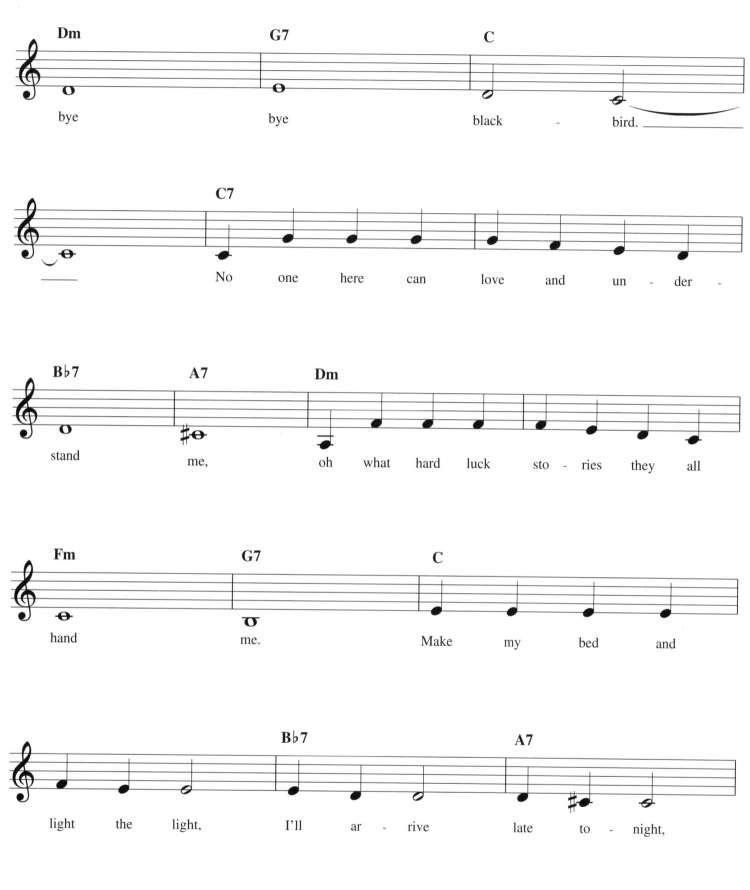

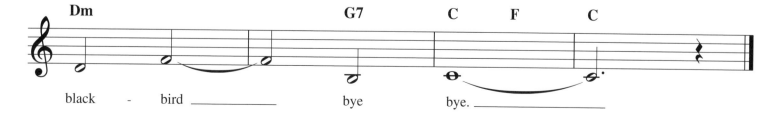

CALL ME IRRESPONSIBLE
from the Paramount Picture PAPA'S DELICATE CONDITION

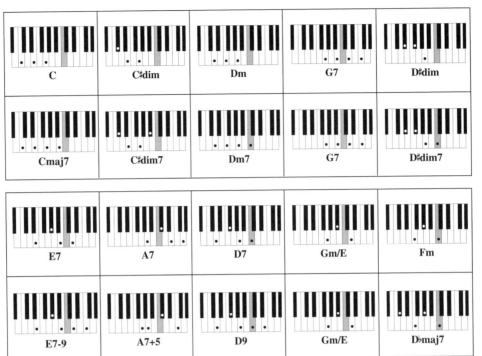

Copyright © 1962, 1963 (Renewed 1990, 1991) by Paramount Music Corporation
International Copyright Secured   All Rights Reserved

Words by SAMMY CAHN
Music by JAMES VAN HEUSEN

Call me ir - re - spon - si - ble, call me

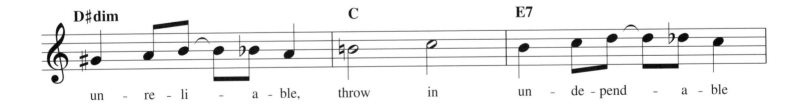

un - re - li - a - ble, throw in un - de - pend - a - ble

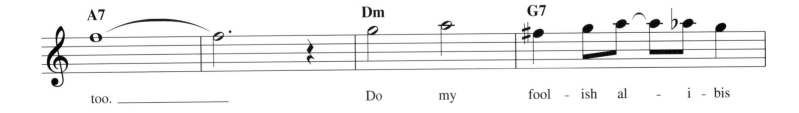

too. _____ Do my fool - ish al - i - bis

CAN YOU FEEL THE LOVE TONIGHT
from Walt Disney Pictures' THE LION KING

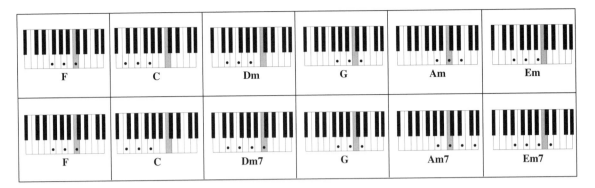

© 1994 Wonderland Music Company, Inc.
All Rights Reserved   Used by Permission

Music by ELTON JOHN
Lyrics by TIM RICE

There's a calm sur - ren - der _____ to the rush of day,
There's a time for ev - 'ry - one if they on - ly learn

when the heat of the roll - ing world can be turned a - way.
that the twist - ing ka - lei - do - scope moves us all in turn.

An en - chant - ed mo - ment, and it sees me through.
There's a rhyme and rea - son to the great out - doors

It's e - nough for this rest - less war - ri - or just to be with you. } And
when the heart of this star - crossed vo - ya - ger beats in time with yours. }

can you feel the love to-night? It is where we are.

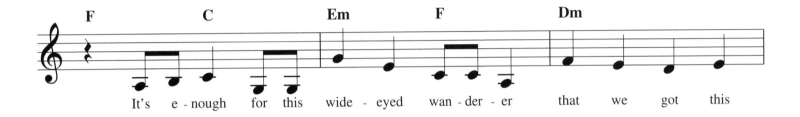

It's e-nough for this wide-eyed wan-der-er that we got this

far. And can you feel the love to-night,

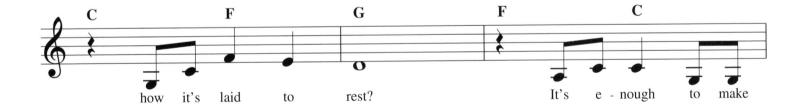

how it's laid to rest? It's e-nough to make

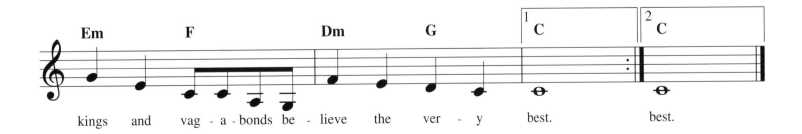

kings and vag-a-bonds be-lieve the ver-y best. best.

CRAZY

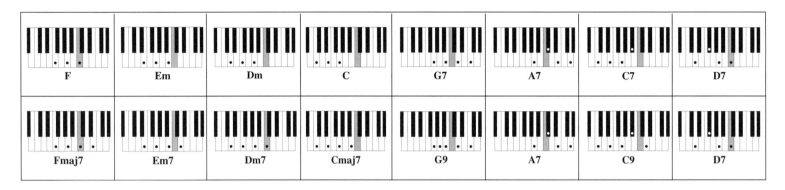

Copyright © 1961 Sony/ATV Songs LLC
Copyright Renewed
All Rights Administered by Sony/ATV Music Publishing,
8 Music Square West, Nashville, TN 37203
International Copyright Secured   All Rights Reserved

Words and Music by
WILLIE NELSON

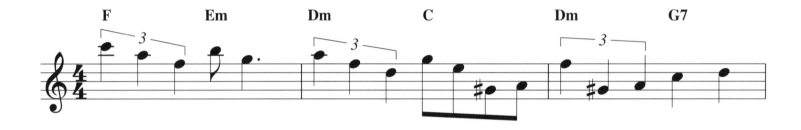

Cra - zy, ___ cra - zy for feel - in' so

lone - ly; ___ I'm cra - zy, ___ cra - zy for feel - in' so

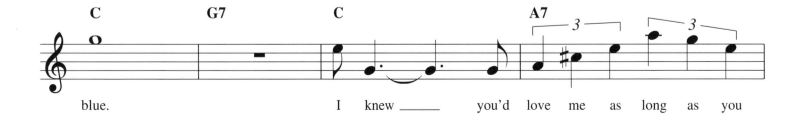

blue. I knew ___ you'd love me as long as you

DON'T GET AROUND MUCH ANYMORE
from SOPHISTICATED LADY

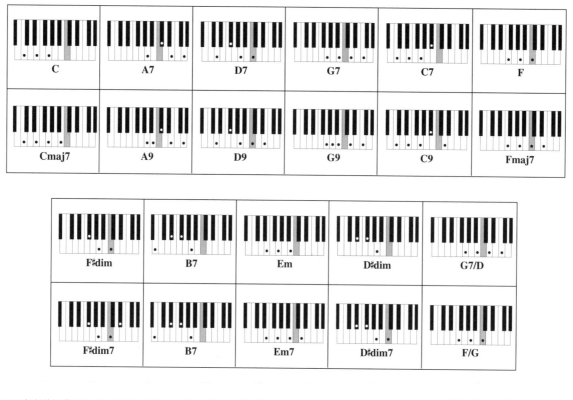

Copyright © 1942 (Renewed 1969) by Famous Music LLC and Harrison Music Corp. in the U.S.A.
Rights for the world outside the U.S.A. Controlled by EMI Robbins Catalog Inc. (Publishing)
and Warner Bros. Publications U.S. Inc. (Print)
International Copyright Secured   All Rights Reserved

Words and Music by DUKE ELLINGTON
and BOB RUSSELL

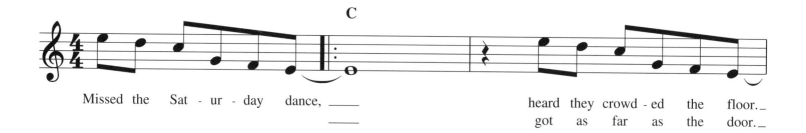

Missed the Sat-ur-day dance, _____ heard they crowd-ed the floor. _
_____ got as far as the door. _

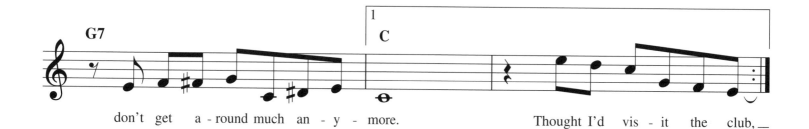

_____ Could-n't bear it with-out you,
They'd have asked me a-bout you,

don't get a-round much an-y-more.   Thought I'd vis-it the club, _

DON'T KNOW MUCH

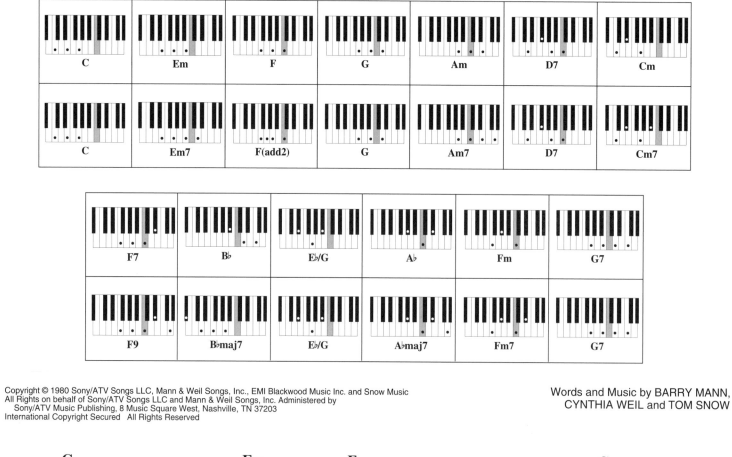

Copyright © 1980 Sony/ATV Songs LLC, Mann & Weil Songs, Inc., EMI Blackwood Music Inc. and Snow Music
All Rights on behalf of Sony/ATV Songs LLC and Mann & Weil Songs, Inc. Administered by
  Sony/ATV Music Publishing, 8 Music Square West, Nashville, TN 37203
International Copyright Secured   All Rights Reserved

Words and Music by BARRY MANN,
CYNTHIA WEIL and TOM SNOW

Look at this face,   I know the years are show-ing.
Look at these eyes,   they've nev-er seen what mat-ters.
(D.C.) Look at this man,   so blessed with in-spi-ra-tion.

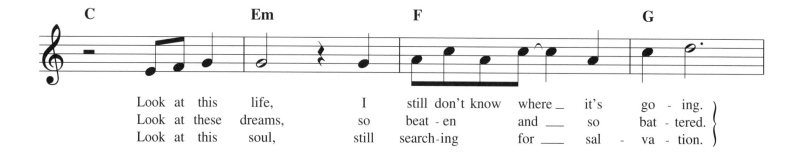

Look at this life,   I still don't know where __ it's go-ing.
Look at these dreams,   so beat-en and __ so bat-tered.
Look at this soul,   still search-ing for __ sal-va-tion.

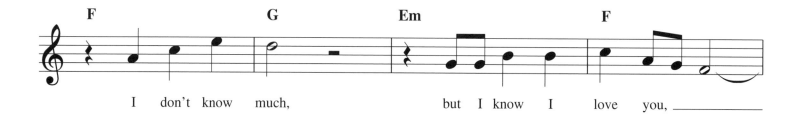

I don't know much,   but I know I love you, _____

and that may be _____ all I need _____ to know. _____

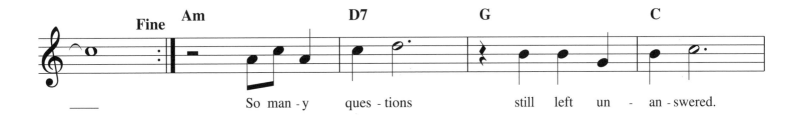

_____ So man-y ques-tions still left un - an - swered.

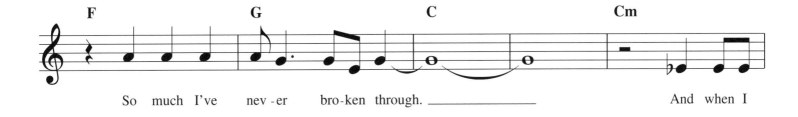

So much I've nev-er bro-ken through. _____ And when I

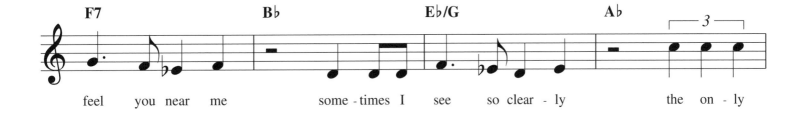

feel you near me some-times I see so clear-ly the on-ly

truth I've ev-er known is me and you. _____

ENDLESS LOVE

from ENDLESS LOVE

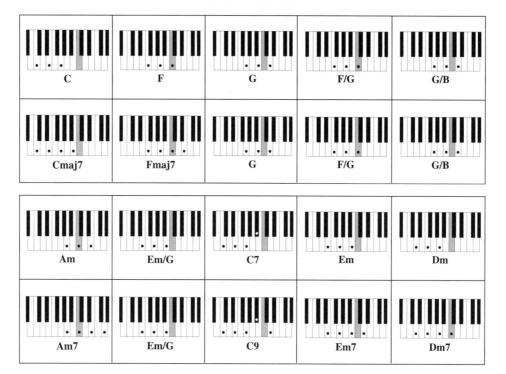

Copyright © 1981 by PGP Music, Brockman Music and Brenda Richie Publishing
All Rights for PGP Music Administered by Intersong U.S.A., Inc.
International Copyright Secured   All Rights Reserved

Words and Music by
LIONEL RICHIE

My love, __ there's on - ly you in my life __ the on - ly
Two hearts, _ two hearts that beat as __ one __ our lives have

thing that's right. __ My first __ love, __ you're ev - 'ry
just be - gun. __ For - ev - er ____ I hold you

breath __ that I take, __ you're ev - 'ry step I make. __ And
close __ in my arms, _ I can't re - sist your charms. _ And

I, ____ I ____ want to share all my love ____
(D.S.) love, ____ I'd __ be a fool for __ you, __ I'm

To Coda ⊕ **C7**

F | F/G | G C | C7

_____ with you; _____ no one else will do. _____ And your eyes,
sure. you _ know I don't mind, _ 'cause

F | F/G | G | **1** C G/B Am Em/G

_____ they tell me how much you care. _____ Oh _____
you, _____ you mean the

F | Em | Dm F/G | **3**

yes, _ you will al - ways be _____ my end - less

C

love. _____

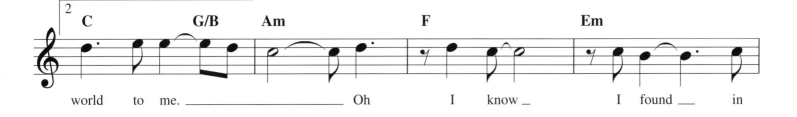

2 C G/B Am | F | Em

world to me. _____ Oh I know _ I found _ in

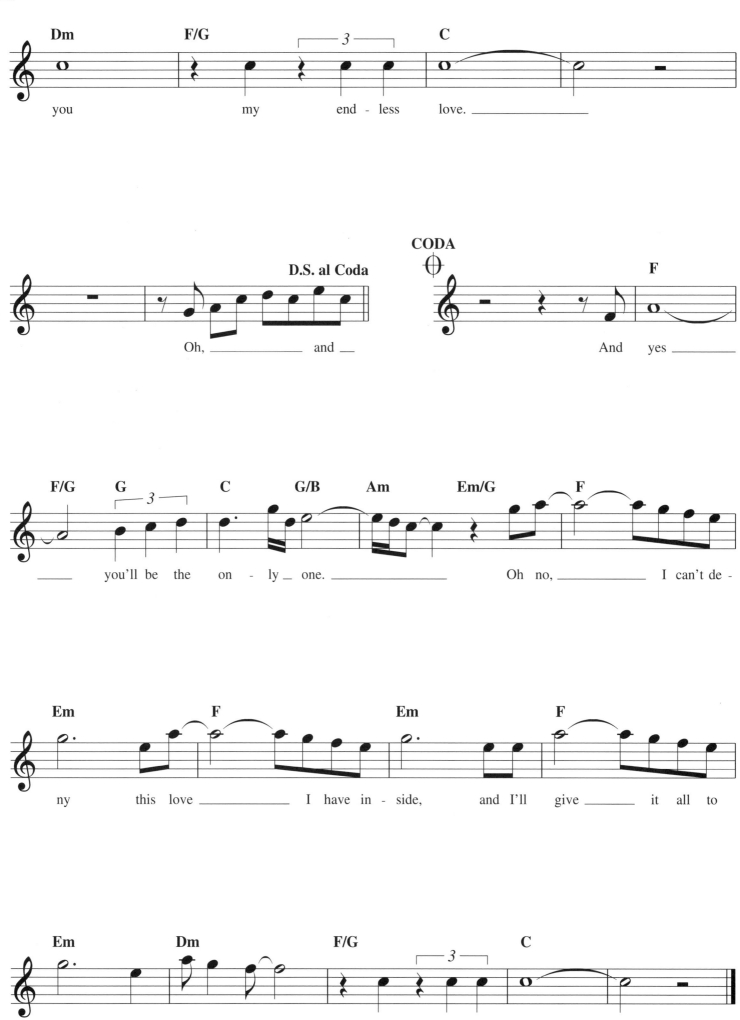

I WILL REMEMBER YOU
Theme from THE BROTHERS McMULLEN

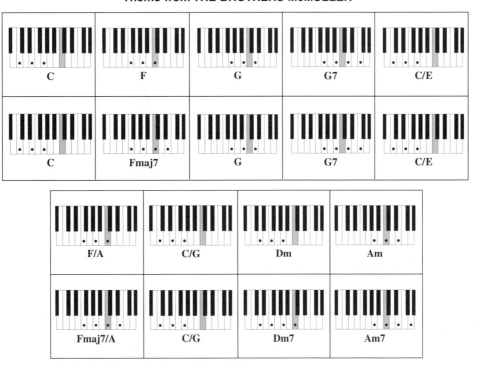

Copyright © 1995 Sony/ATV Songs LLC, Tyde Music, Seamus Egan Music
and TCF Music Publishing, Inc.
All Rights on behalf of Sony/ATV Songs LLC and Tyde Music Administered by
Sony/ATV Music Publishing, 8 Music Square West, Nashville, TN 37203
All Rights on behalf of Seamus Egan Music Administered by
Fox Film Music Corp.
International Copyright Secured   All Rights Reserved

Words and Music by SARAH McLACHLAN,
SEAMUS EGAN and DAVE MERENDA

I will re-mem-ber you, _____ Will you re-mem-ber me? _

_____ Don't let your life _____ pass _ you by. _____

Weep not for _____ the mem - o - ries, _____ Re -

mem - ber the good times that we had. _____ We
I'm so tired, but I can't sleep. ___
so a - fraid to love you, more a - fraid to lose,

28

let them slip a - way from us when things got _____ bad. _____
Stand - in' on the edge of some - thing much too _____ deep. _____ It's
cling - ing to a past that does - n't let me _____ choose. _ Well,

Clear - ly I first saw you _____ smil - in' in the sun. Wan - na
fun - ny how I feel so much but I can - not say a word. We are
once there was a dark - ness, a deep and end - less night. You

feel your warmth up - on me. I wan - na be the one. _____
scream - ing in - side or we can't be heard.
gave me ev - 'ry - thing you had oh, you gave me light. _____

I will re - mem - ber you, _____ Will you re - mem - ber me? _

_____ Don't let your life ___ pass ___ you by. _____

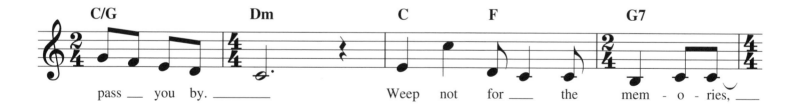

FLY ME TO THE MOON
(In Other Words)
featured in the Motion Picture ONCE AROUND

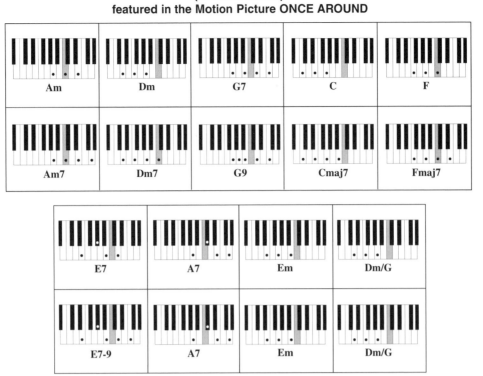

TRO - © Copyright 1954 (Renewed) Hampshire House Publishing Corp., New York, NY
International Copyright Secured
All Rights Reserved Including Public Performance For Profit
Used by Permission

Words and Music by
BART HOWARD

Am   **Dm**   **G7**

Fly me to the moon, and let me play a - mong the

C   **F**   **Dm**

stars; let me see what spring is like on

E7   **Am**   **A7**   **Dm**

Ju - pi - ter and Mars. In oth - er words, _____

G7   **C**   **Am**

_____ hold my hand! _____ In

Dm   **G7**   **C**

oth - er words, _____ dar - ling kiss me! _____

GEORGIA ON MY MIND

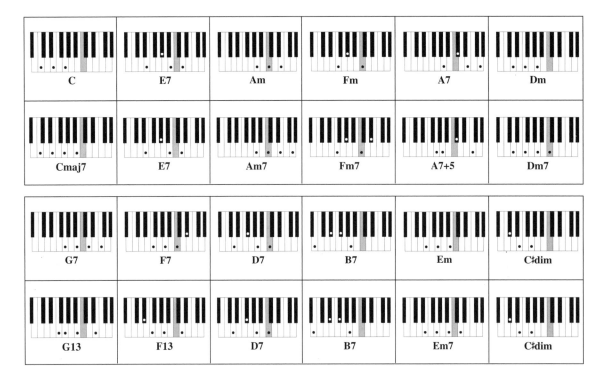

Copyright © 1930 by Peermusic III, Ltd.
Copyright Renewed
International Copyright Secured   All Rights Reserved

Words by STUART GORRELL
Music by HOAGY CARMICHAEL

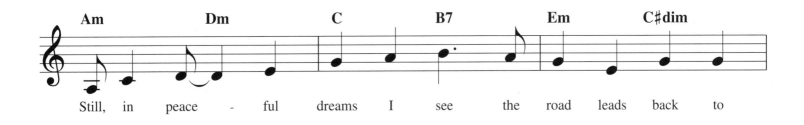

out to me, ___ oth - er eyes ___ smile ten - der - ly. ___

Still, in peace - ful dreams I see the road leads back to

you. _____ Geor - gia, _____ Geor - gia, _____

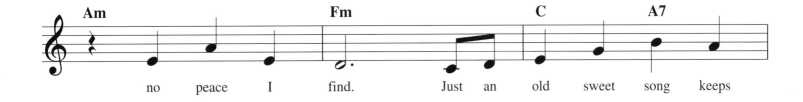

no peace I find. Just an old sweet song keeps

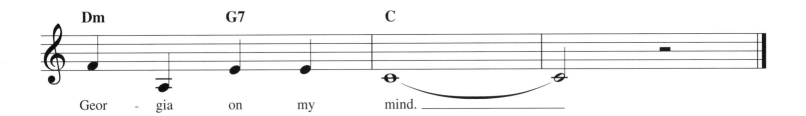

Geor - gia on my mind. _____

THE GIRL FROM IPANEMA
(Garôta de Ipanema)

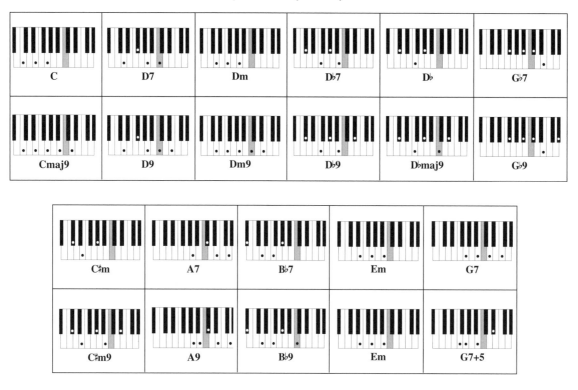

Copyright © 1963 ANTONIO CARLOS JOBIM and VINICIUS DE MORAES, Brazil
Copyright Renewed 1991 and Assigned to SONGS OF UNIVERSAL, INC. and NEW THUNDER MUSIC, INC.
English Words Renewed 1991 by NORMAN GIMBEL for the World and Assigned to NEW THUNDER MUSIC, INC.
Administered by GIMBEL MUSIC GROUP, INC. (P.O. Box 15221, Beverly Hills, CA 90209-1221 USA)
All Rights Reserved   Used by Permission

Music by ANTONIO CARLOS JOBIM
English Words by NORMAN GIMBEL
Original Words by VINICIUS DE MORAES

Moderate Bossa Nova

Tall   and tan and   young and love - ly, the   girl from I pa - ne -
When   she walks she's like   a   sam - ba that swings so   cool and sways

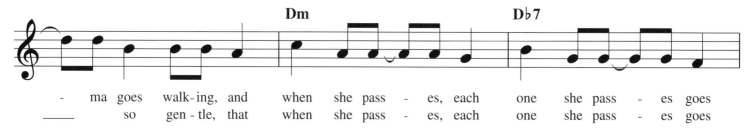

- ma goes walk-ing, and   when she pass - es, each   one she pass - es goes
____ so gen - tle, that   when she pass - es, each   one she pass - es goes

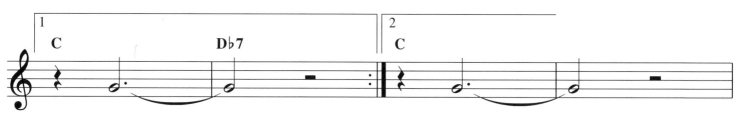

"a - a - h!" ____   "a - a - h!" ____

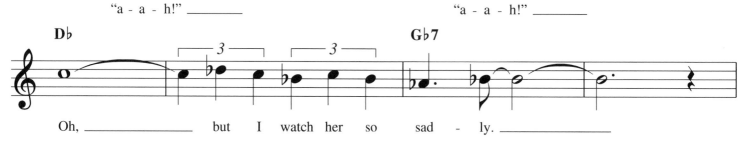

Oh, ____   but I watch her so sad - ly. ____

GOD BLESS' THE CHILD
from BUBBLING BROWN SUGAR
featured in the Motion Picture LADY SINGS THE BLUES

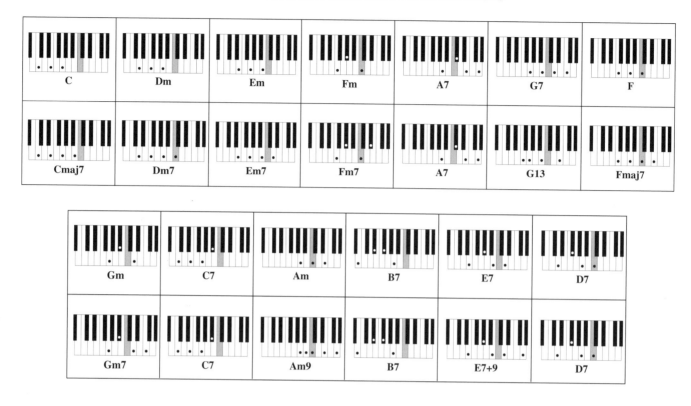

Copyright © 1941 by Edward B. Marks Music Company
Copyright Renewed
International Copyright Secured   All Rights Reserved
Used by Permission

Words and Music by ARTHUR HERZOG JR.
and BILLIE HOLIDAY

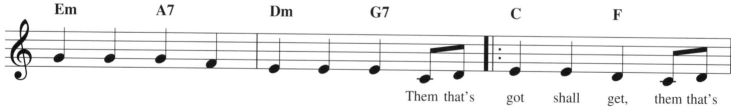

Them that's got shall get, them that's

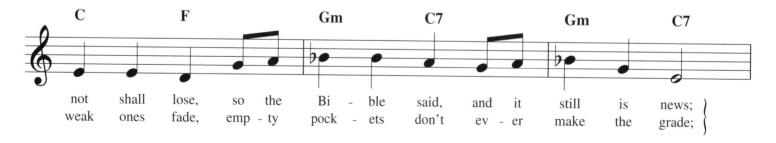

not shall lose, so the Bi - ble said, and it still is news;
weak ones fade, emp - ty pock - ets don't ev - er make the grade;

Ma - ma may have, Pa - pa may have, but God bless' the child that's

GREAT BALLS OF FIRE

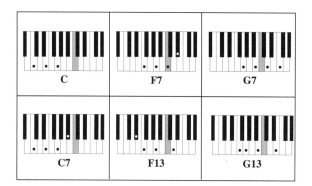

Copyright © 1957 by Chappell & Co. and Unichappell Music Inc.
Copyright Renewed
International Copyright Secured   All Rights Reserved

Words and Music by OTIS BLACKWELL
and JACK HAMMER

You shake my nerves and you rat-tle my brain. _ Too much love drives a man in-sane. _ You broke my will, but what a thrill. Good-ness gra-cious, great _ balls of fire! I laughed at love 'cause I thought it was fun-ny. You came a-long and you moved _ me, hon-ey. I changed my mind,

HEART AND SOUL
from the Paramount Short Subject A SONG IS BORN

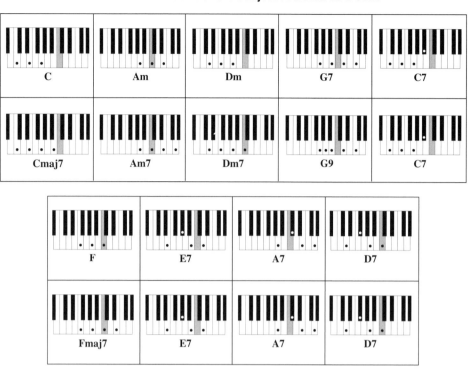

Copyright © 1938 (Renewed 1965) by Famous Music LLC
International Copyright Secured All Rights Reserved

Words by FRANK LOESSER
Music by HOAGY CARMICHAEL

HERE, THERE AND EVERYWHERE

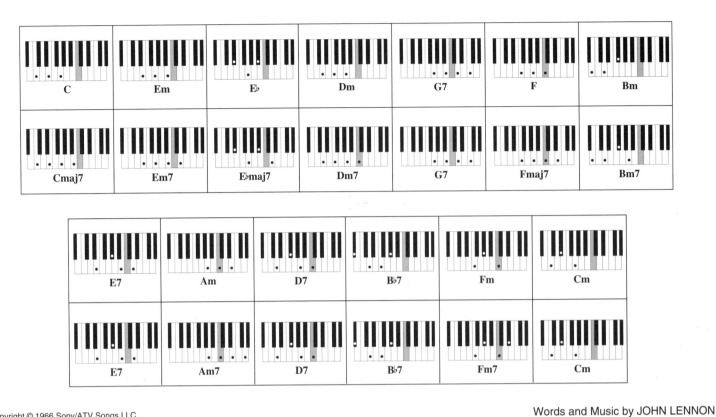

Copyright © 1966 Sony/ATV Songs LLC
Copyright Renewed
All Rights Administered by Sony/ATV Music Publishing,
  8 Music Square West, Nashville, TN 37203
International Copyright Secured   All Rights Reserved

Words and Music by JOHN LENNON
and PAUL McCARTNEY

C   **Em**   **E♭**

To lead a bet-ter life I need my love to be here. _

Dm   **G7**   **C**   **Dm**   **Em**   **F**

_ Here, mak-ing each day _ of the year,
There, run-ning my hands _ through her hair, _

C   **Dm**   **Em**   **F**   **Bm**   **E7**

_ chang-ing my life _ with a wave _ of her hand. _
_ both of us think-ing how good _ it can be. _

Bm   **E7**   **Am**   **D7**   **1.** **Dm**   **G7**

No-bod-y can _ de-ny _ that there's some-thing there. _
Some-one is speak-ing, but _ she does-n't know he's there. _

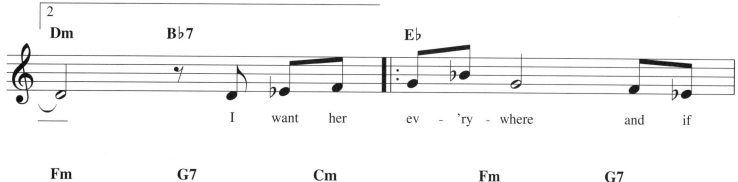

I want her ev - 'ry - where and if

she's be - side me I know I need nev - er care. But to love her is to need her

ev - 'ry - where, __ know - ing that love __ is to share; __

each one be - liev - ing that love __ nev - er dies, __

watch - ing her eyes __ and hop - ing I'm al - ways there. __

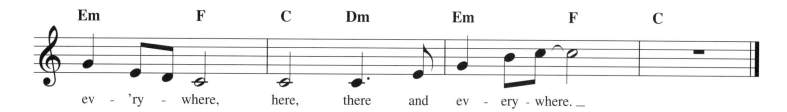

I want her __ I will be there and

ev - 'ry - where, here, there and ev - ery - where. __

HEY JUDE

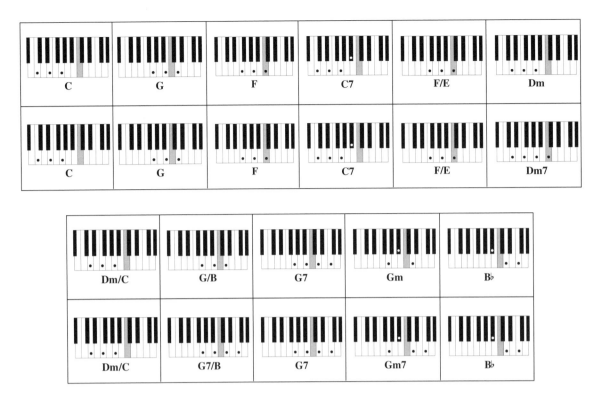

Copyright © 1968 Sony/ATV Songs LLC
Copyright Renewed
All Rights Administered by Sony/ATV Music Publishing,
8 Music Square West, Nashville, TN 37203
International Copyright Secured   All Rights Reserved

Words and Music by JOHN LENNON
and PAUL McCARTNEY

Hey Jude, _____ don't make it bad. Take a
sad song _____ and make it bet - ter. _____ Re -
mem - ber to let her in - to your heart. Then you can start _____
_____ to make it bet - ter. (Hey)

Jude, _____ don't be a - fraid.
Jude, _____ don't let me down.

You were made to _____ go out and
You have found her, _____ now go and

HOUND DOG

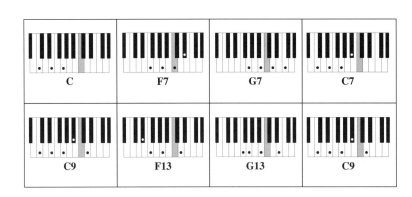

Copyright © 1956 by Elvis Presley Music, Inc. and Lion Publishing Co., Inc.
Copyright Renewed, Assigned to Gladys Music and Universal Music Corp.
All Rights Administered by Cherry Lane Music Publishing Company, Inc. and Chrysalis Music
International Copyright Secured   All Rights Reserved

Words and Music by JERRY LEIBER
and MIKE STOLLER

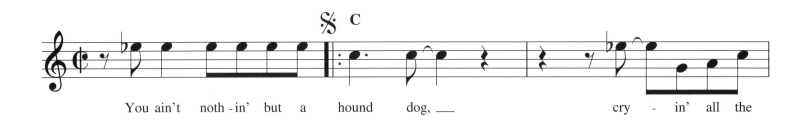

You ain't noth-in' but a hound dog, ___ cry - in' all the

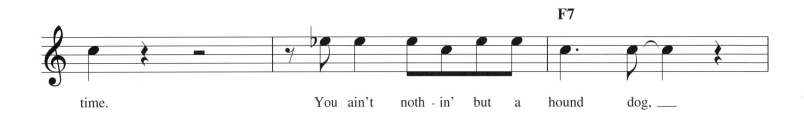

time. You ain't noth-in' but a hound dog, ___

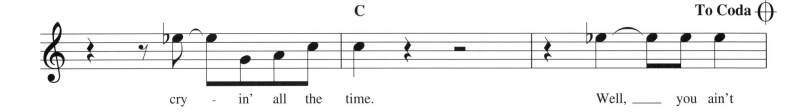

cry - in' all the time. Well, ___ you ain't

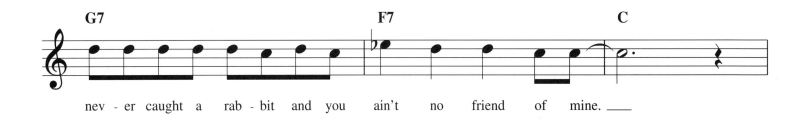

nev - er caught a rab - bit and you ain't no friend of mine. ___

HOW SWEET IT IS
(To Be Loved by You)

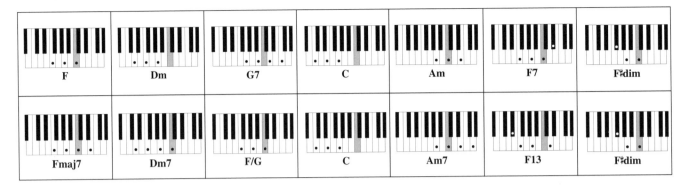

© 1964 (Renewed 1992) JOBETE MUSIC CO., INC.
All Rights Controlled and Administered by EMI BLACKWOOD MUSIC INC.
on behalf of STONE AGATE MUSIC (A Division of JOBETE MUSIC CO., INC.)
All Rights Reserved   International Copyright Secured   Used by Permission

Words and Music by EDWARD HOLLAND,
LAMONT DOZIER and BRIAN HOLLAND

I LEFT MY HEART IN SAN FRANCISCO

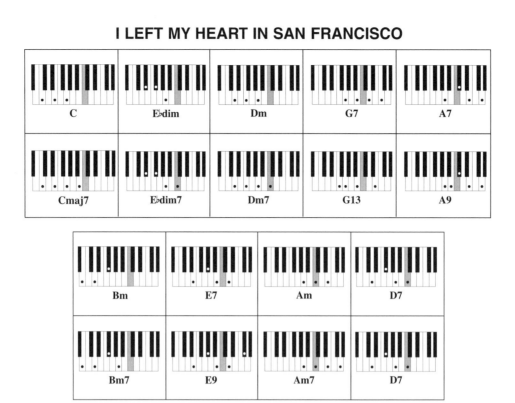

© 1954 (Renewed 1982) COLGEMS-EMI MUSIC INC.
All Rights Reserved   International Copyright Secured   Used by Permission

Words by DOUGLASS CROSS
Music by GEORGE CORY

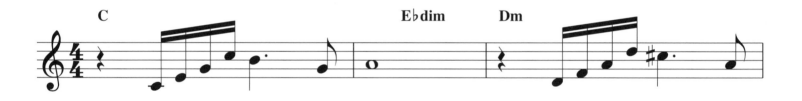

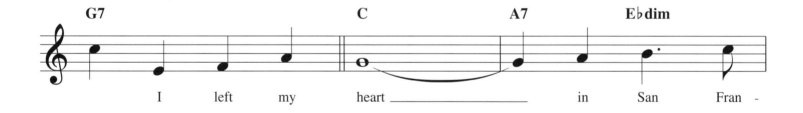

I left my heart ___ in San Fran-

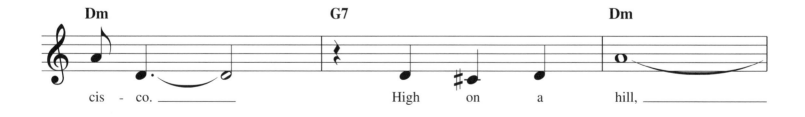

cis-co. ___ High on a hill, ___

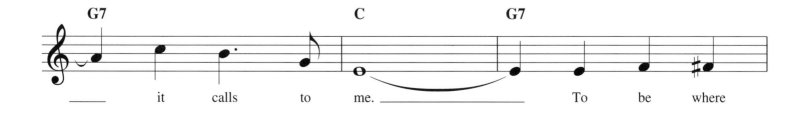

___ it calls to me. ___ To be where

lit - tle ca - ble cars _____ climb half - way to the stars _____

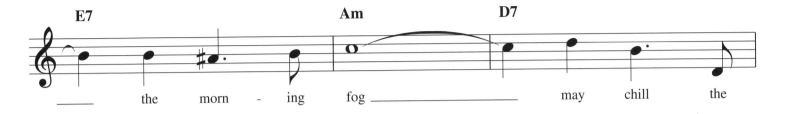

_____ the morn - ing fog _____ may chill the

air I don't care! My love waits there _____

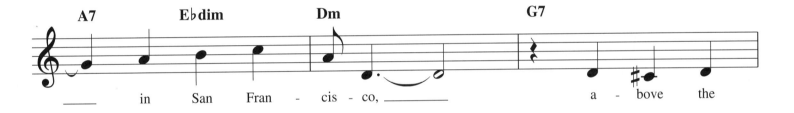

_____ in San Fran - cis - co, _____ a - bove the

blue _____ and wind - y sea. _____ When I come

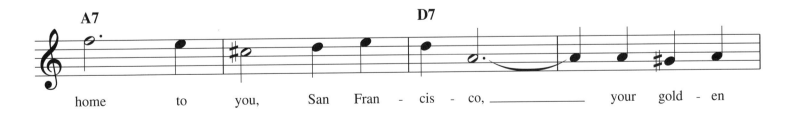

home to you, San Fran - cis - co, _____ your gold - en

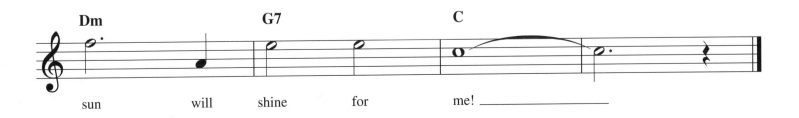

sun will shine for me! _____

I'VE GOT YOU UNDER MY SKIN
from BORN TO DANCE

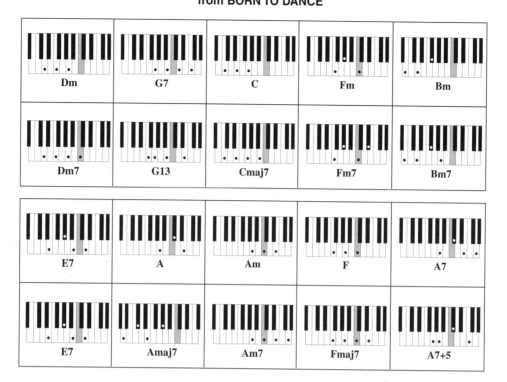

Copyright © 1936 by Chappell & Co.
Copyright Renewed, Assigned to John F. Wharton, Trustee of the
  Cole Porter Musical and Literary Property Trusts
Chappell & Co. owner of publication and allied rights throughout the world
International Copyright Secured   All Rights Reserved

Words and Music by
COLE PORTER

I've got you _____ un-der my skin. _____ I've

got you _____ deep in the heart of me, _____

_____ so deep in my heart, _____ you're real-ly a

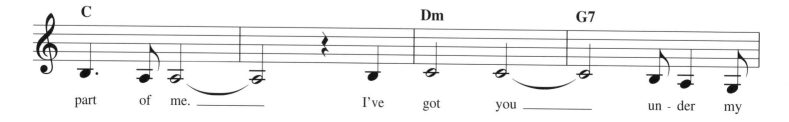

part of me. _____ I've got you _____ un-der my

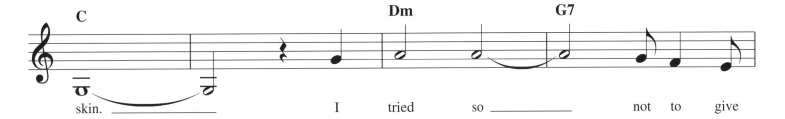

skin. _____ I tried so _____ not to give

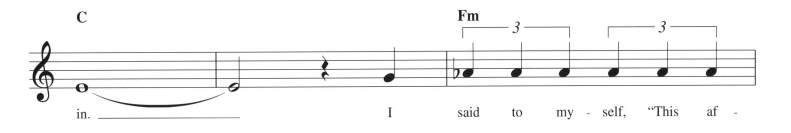

in. _____ I said to my-self, "This af -

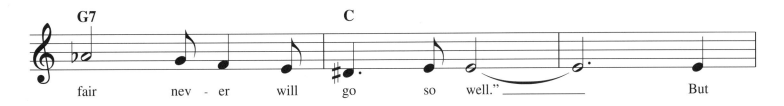

fair nev-er will go so well." _____ But

why should I try to re-sist when, dar-ling, I know so well _____

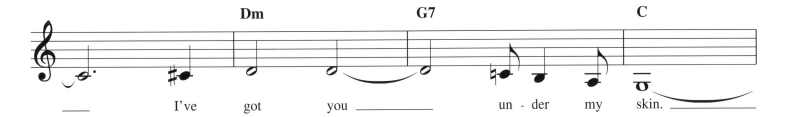

_____ I've got you _____ un-der my skin. _____

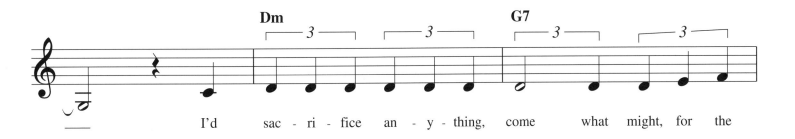

I'd sac-ri-fice an-y-thing, come what might, for the

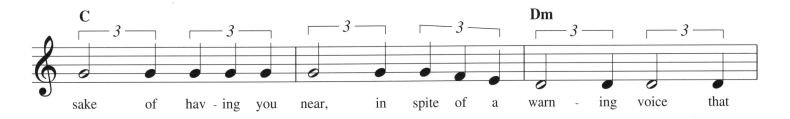

sake of hav-ing you near, in spite of a warn-ing voice that

LET IT BE

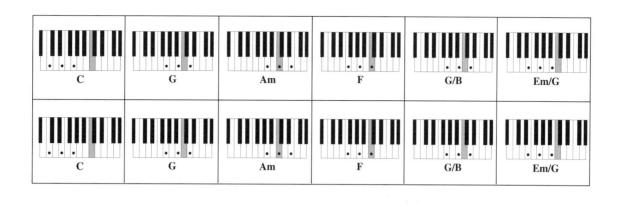

Copyright © 1970 Sony/ATV Songs LLC
Copyright Renewed
All Rights Administered by Sony/ATV Music Publishing,
  8 Music Square West, Nashville, TN 37203
International Copyright Secured   All Rights Reserved

Words and Music by JOHN LENNON
and PAUL McCARTNEY

When I find my-self in times of trou-ble Moth-er Ma-ry comes to me,
when the bro-ken-heart-ed peo-ple liv-ing in the world a-gree,

speak-ing words of wis-dom, let it be. _____ And
there will be an an-swer, let it be. _____ For

in my hour of dark-ness she is stand-ing right in front of me. Speak-ing words of wis-dom, let it
though they may be part-ed, there is still a chance that they will see. There will be an an-swer, let it

be. ___
be. ___ Let it be, let it be, ___ let it be, ___ let it be.

Whis-per words of wis-dom, let it be. _____ And
There will be an an-swer, let it be. _____

IF

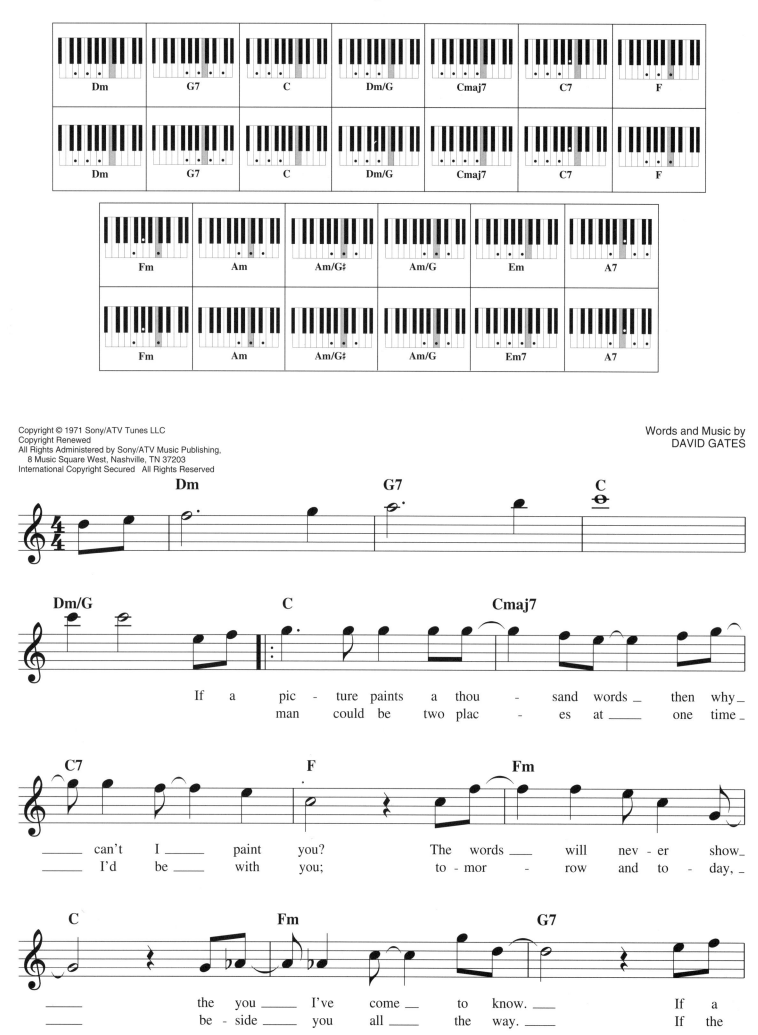

Copyright © 1971 Sony/ATV Tunes LLC
Copyright Renewed
All Rights Administered by Sony/ATV Music Publishing,
  8 Music Square West, Nashville, TN 37203
International Copyright Secured   All Rights Reserved

Words and Music by
DAVID GATES

If a pic - ture paints a thou - sand words _ then why _
man could be two plac - es at ___ one time _

_____ can't I _____ paint you? The words ___ will nev - er show _
_____ I'd be ___ paint with you; to - mor - row and to - day,

_____ the you ___ I've come _ to know. ___ If a
_____ be - side ___ you all ___ the way. ___ If the

IMAGINE

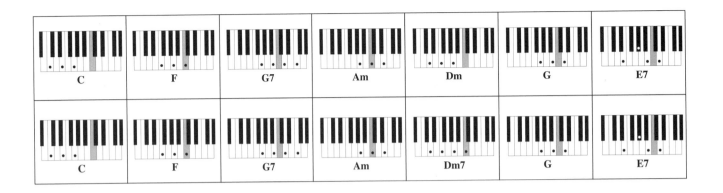

© 1971 (Renewed 1999) LENONO.MUSIC
All Rights Controlled and Administered by EMI BLACKWOOD MUSIC INC.
All Rights Reserved   International Copyright Secured   Used by Permission

Words and Music by
JOHN LENNON

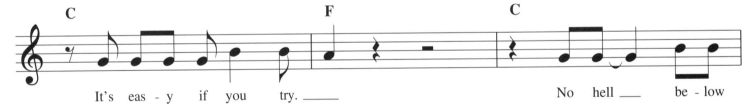

I - mag - ine there's   no   heav - en.

It's eas - y   if   you   try. _____   No hell ___   be - low

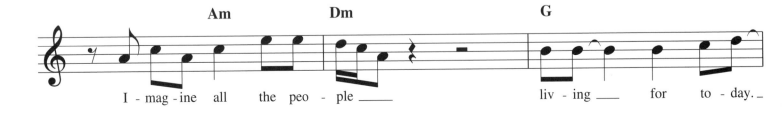

us,   a - bove us on - ly sky.

I - mag - ine all   the peo - ple ___   liv - ing ___ for to - day. __

IN A SENTIMENTAL MOOD

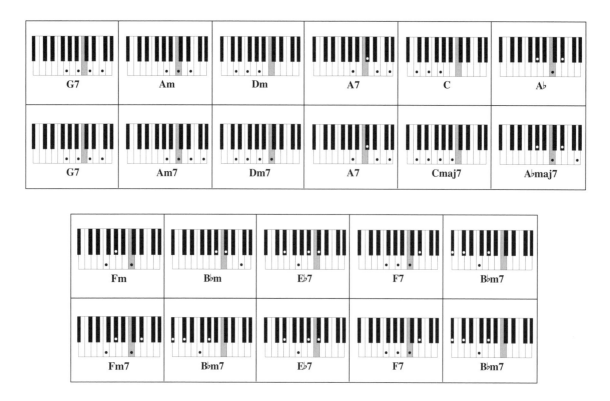

Copyright © 1935 (Renewed 1963) and Assigned to Famous Music LLC and EMI Mills Music Inc. in the U.S.A.
Rights for the world outside the U.S.A. Controlled by EMI Mills Music Inc. (Publishing) and Warner Bros. Publications U.S. Inc. (Print)
International Copyright Secured   All Rights Reserved

Words and Music by DUKE ELLINGTON,
IRVING MILLS and MANNY KURTZ

In a sen-ti-men-tal

mood, _____ I can see the stars come through my room, _____

_____ while your lov-ing at-ti-tude _____ is like a frame that

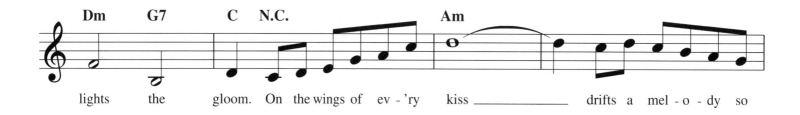

lights the gloom. On the wings of ev-'ry kiss _____ drifts a mel-o-dy so

ISN'T IT ROMANTIC?

from the Paramount Picture LOVE ME TONIGHT

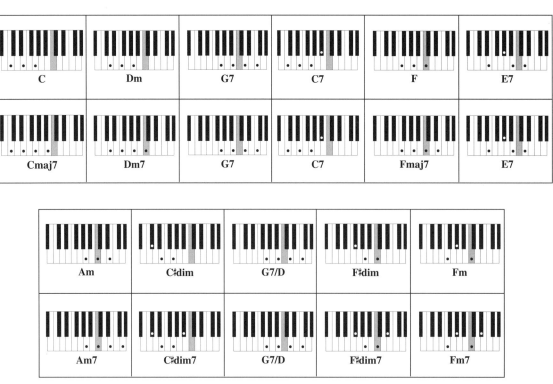

Copyright © 1932 (Renewed 1959) by Famous Music LLC
International Copyright Secured   All Rights Reserved

Words by LORENZ HART
Music by RICHARD RODGERS

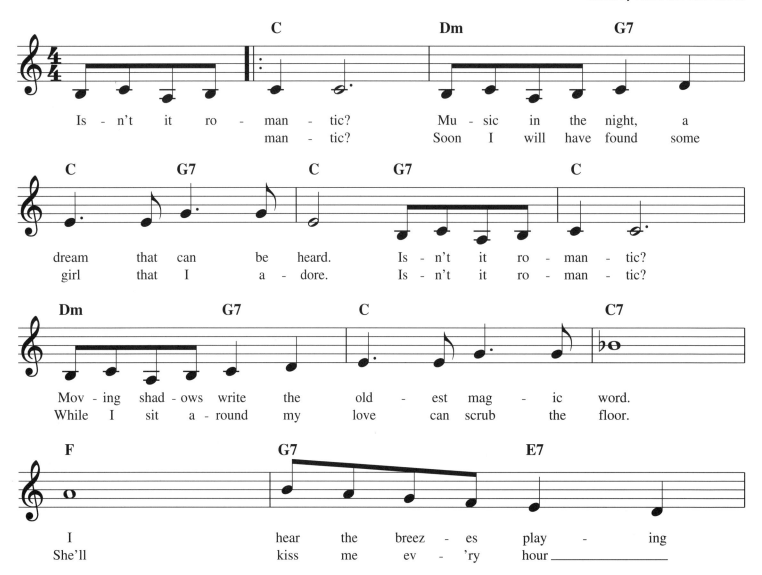

Is - n't it ro - man - tic? Mu - sic in the night, a
man - tic? Soon I will have found some

dream that can be heard. Is - n't it ro - man - tic?
girl that I a - dore. Is - n't it ro - man - tic?

Mov - ing shad - ows write the old - est mag - ic word.
While I sit a - round my love can scrub the floor.

I hear the breez - es play - ing
She'll kiss me ev - 'ry hour _____

IT'S ONLY A PAPER MOON
from the Musical Production THE GREAT MAGOO

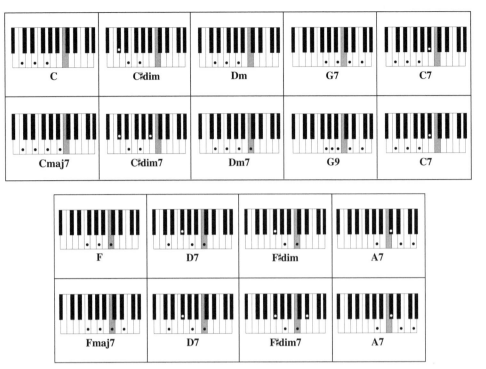

© 1933 (Renewed) CHAPPELL & CO., GLOCCA MORRA MUSIC and S.A. MUSIC CO.
All Rights Reserved

Lyric by BILLY ROSE and E.Y. HARBURG
Music by HAROLD ARLEN

Say, it's on-ly a pa-per moon __ sail-ing o-ver a
Yes, it's on-ly a can-vas sky ____ hang-ing o-ver a

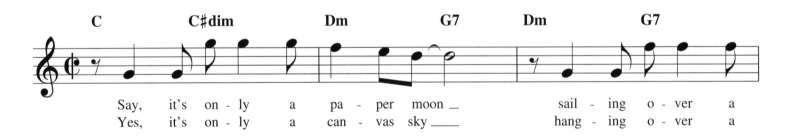

card-board sea, ___ but it would-n't be make-be-lieve ___ if you __
mus-lin tree, ___

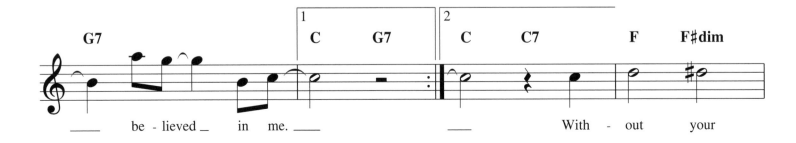

___ be-lieved ___ in me. ___   With - out your

JAILHOUSE ROCK

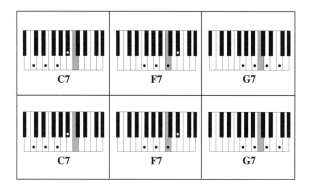

© 1957 (Renewed) JERRY LEIBER MUSIC and MIKE STOLLER MUSIC
All Rights Reserved

Words and Music by JERRY LEIBER
and MIKE STOLLER

1. The war-den threw a par-ty in the
2. - 5. *(See additional lyrics)*

coun-ty jail. The pris-on band was there and they be-gan to wail. The

band was jump-in' and the joint be-gan to swing. You should have heard those knocked-out

Chorus

jail-birds sing. Let's rock! Ev-'ry-bod-y let's

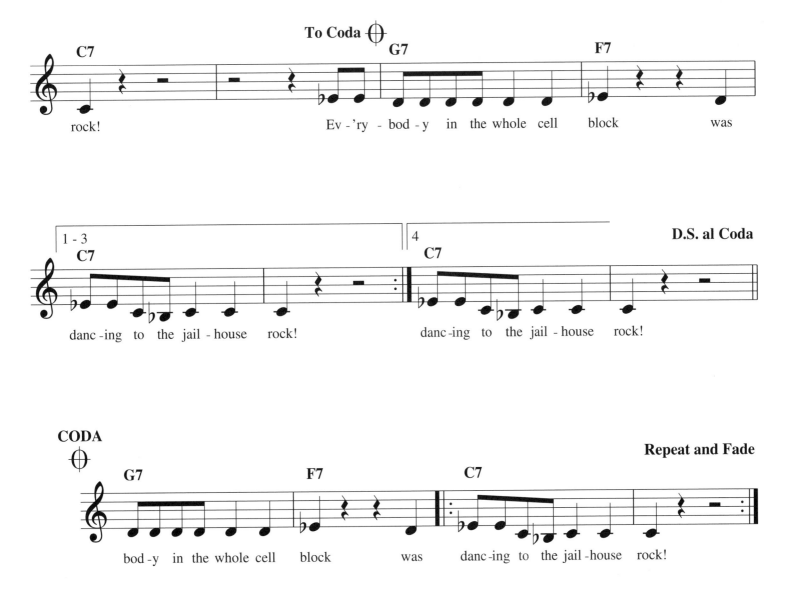

Additional Lyrics

2. Spider Murphy played the tenor saxophone
   Little Joe was blowin' on the slide trombone,
   The drummer boy from Illinois went crash, boom, bang;
   The whole rhythm section was the Purple Gang.
   (Chorus)

3. Number Forty-seven said to number Three;
   "You're the cutest jailbird I ever did see.
   I sure would be delighted with your company,
   Come on and do the Jailhouse Rock with me."
   (Chorus)

4. The sad sack was a-sittin' on a block of stone,
   Way over in the corner weeping all alone.
   The warden said: "Hey Buddy, don't you be so square,
   If you can't find a partner, use a wooden chair!"
   (Chorus)

5. Shifty Henry said to Bugs: "For heaven's sake,
   No one's lookin', now's our chance to make a break."
   Bugsy turned to Shifty and he said: "Nix, nix;
   I wanna stick around awhile and get my kicks."
   (Chorus)

KANSAS CITY

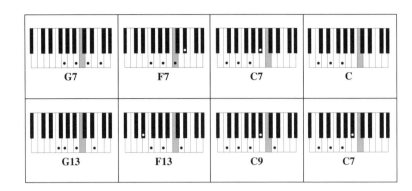

© 1952 (Renewed) JERRY LEIBER MUSIC, MIKE STOLLER MUSIC
and NANCY NATHAN GOLDSTEIN
All Rights Reserved

Words and Music by JERRY LEIBER
and MIKE STOLLER

MICHELLE

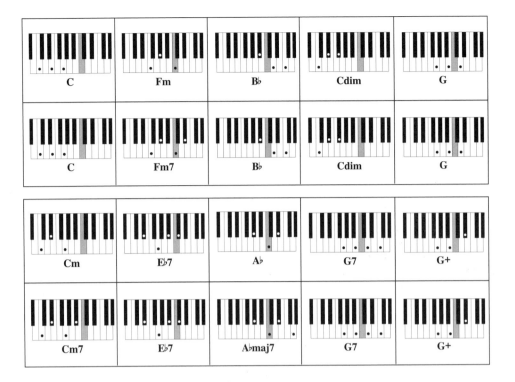

Copyright © 1965 Sony/ATV Songs LLC
Copyright Renewed
All Rights Administered by Sony/ATV Music Publishing, 8 Music Square West, Nashville, TN 37203
International Copyright Secured   All Rights Reserved

Words and Music by JOHN LENNON
and PAUL McCARTNEY

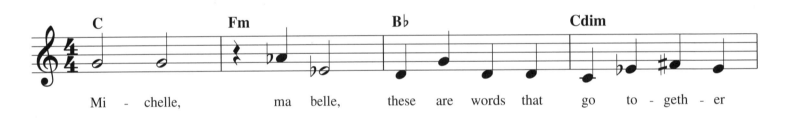

Mi - chelle,   ma belle,   these are words that go to - geth - er

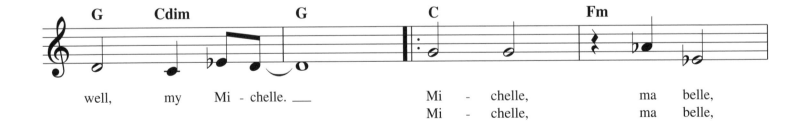

well,   my Mi - chelle. ___   Mi - chelle,   ma belle,
Mi - chelle,   ma belle,

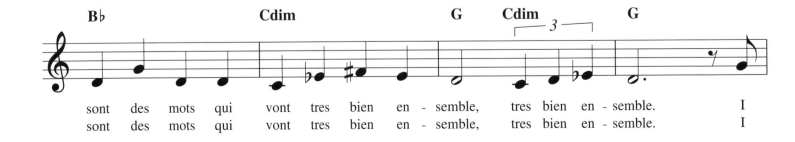

sont des mots qui vont tres bien en - semble,   tres bien en - semble.   I
sont des mots qui vont tres bien en - semble,   tres bien en - semble.   I

72

MANDY

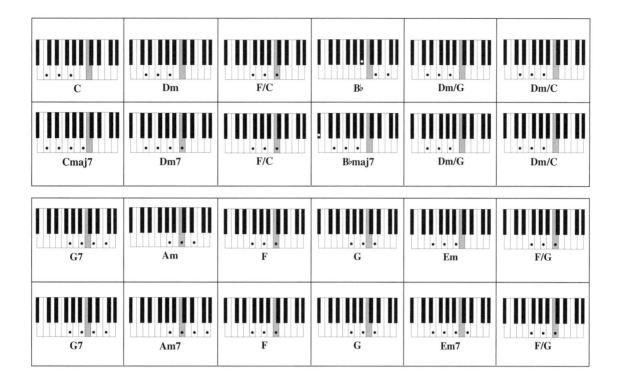

Copyright © 1971 by Graphle Music Ltd. and Screen Gems-EMI Music Inc.
Copyright Renewed
All Rights for Graphle Music Ltd. Administered in the U.S. and Canada by Morris Music, Inc.
International Copyright Secured   All Rights Reserved

Words and Music by SCOTT ENGLISH
and RICHARD KERR

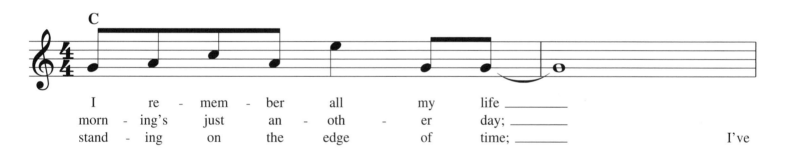

I re- mem- ber all my life _____
morn - ing's just an - oth - er day; _____
stand - ing on the edge of time; _____ I've

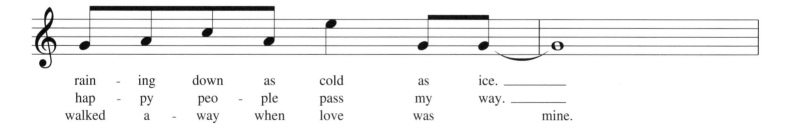

rain - ing down as cold as ice. _____
hap - py peo - ple pass my way. _____
walked a - way when love was mine.

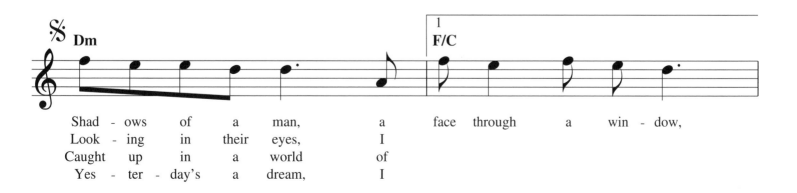

Shad - ows of a man, a face through a win - dow,
Look - ing in their eyes, I
Caught up in a world of
Yes - ter - day's a dream, I

G7

I'm

2

Am   Em   F

Man - dy.   *(Instrumental)*

Dm   G7   **D.S. al Coda**

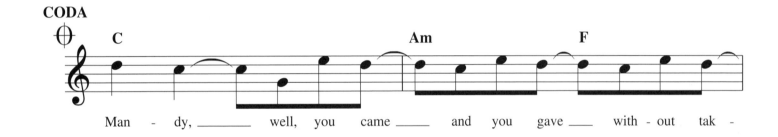

CODA

C   Am   F

Man - dy, _____ well, you came _____ and you gave _____ with - out tak -

G   G7   C

- ing, but I sent _____ you a - way. _ Oh Man - dy, well, you kissed _

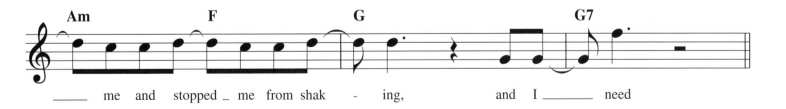

Am   F   G   G7

Repeat and Fade

_____ me and stopped _ me from shak - ing, and I _____ need

C   Am   F   G   F/G

you.   *(Instrumental)*

MISTY

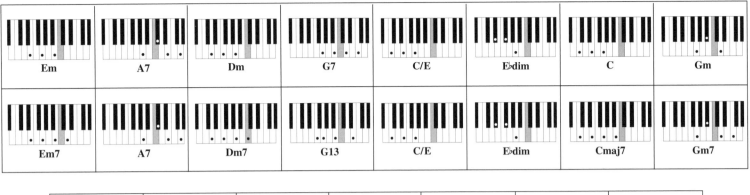

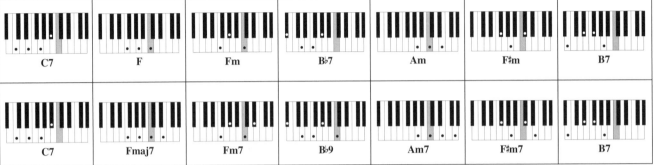

Copyright © 1955 by Octave Music Publishing Corp., Marke Music Publishing Co., Inc.,
    Reganesque Music, Limerick Music and My Dad's Songs, Inc.
Copyright Renewed 1982
All Rights for Marke Music Publishing Co., Inc. Administered by BMG Songs
All Rights for Reganesque Music, Limerick Music and My Dad's Songs, Inc.
    Administered by Spirit Two Music, Inc.
International Copyright Secured   All Rights Reserved

Words by JOHNNY BURKE
Music by ERROLL GARNER

Look at

me,   I'm as   help-less as a   kit-ten up a
way,   and a   thou-sand vi-o-lins be-gin to
own,   would I   wan-der through this won-der-land a-

tree,   and I feel like I'm cling-ing to a cloud,   I
play,   or it might be the   sound of your hel-lo,   that
lone,   nev-er know-ing my   right foot from my left,   my

MOOD INDIGO
from SOPHISTICATED LADIES

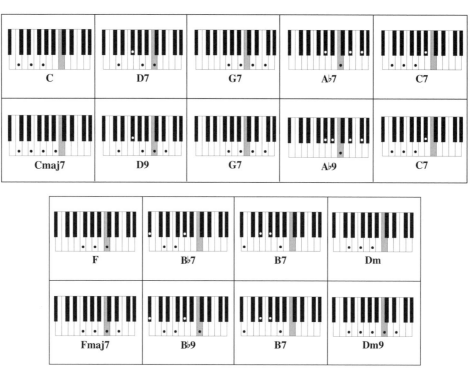

Copyright © 1931 (Renewed 1958) and Assigned to Famous Music LLC,
EMI Mills Music Inc. and Indigo Mood Music c/o The Songwriters Guild Of America in the U.S.A.
Rights for the world outside the U.S.A. Controlled by EMI Mills Music Inc. (Publishing)
and Warner Bros. Publications U.S. Inc. (Print)
International Copyright Secured   All Rights Reserved

Words and Music by DUKE ELLINGTON,
IRVING MILLS and ALBANY BIGARD

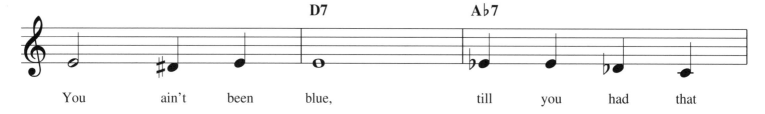

You ain't been blue, no, no, no.

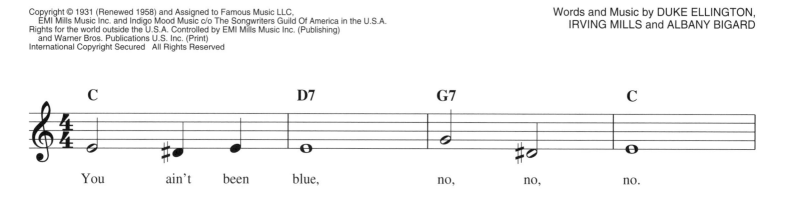

You ain't been blue, till you had that

mood in-di-go. That feel-in' goes steal-in'

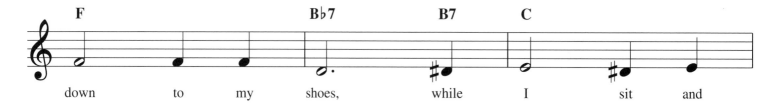

down to my shoes, while I sit and

MOON RIVER
from the Paramount Picture BREAKFAST AT TIFFANY'S

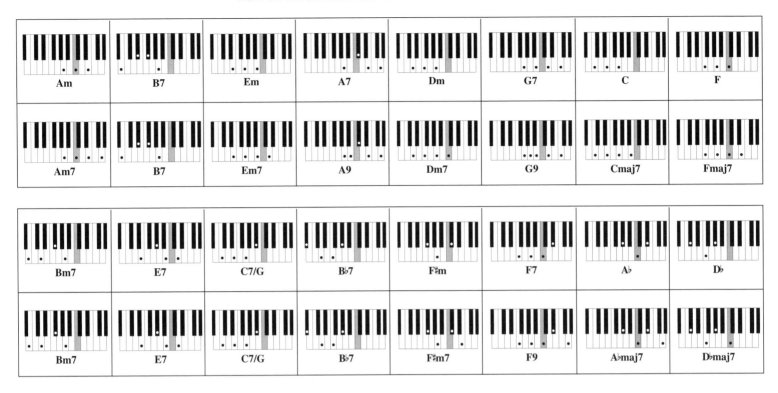

Copyright © 1961 (Renewed 1989) by Famous Music LLC
International Copyright Secured   All Rights Reserved

Words by JOHNNY MERCER
Music by HENRY MANCINI

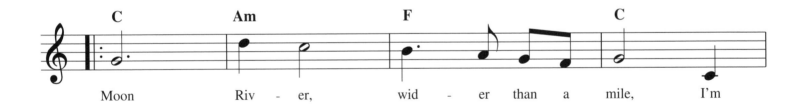

Moon Riv - er, wid - er than a mile, I'm

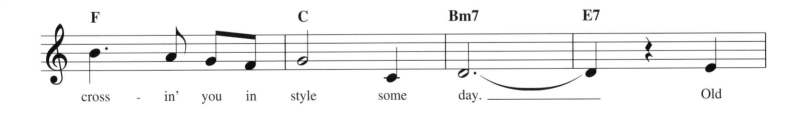

cross - in' you in style some day. _____ Old

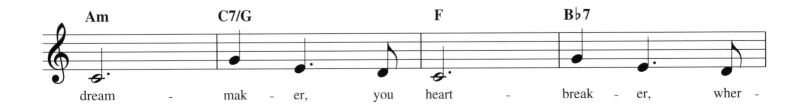

dream - mak - er, you heart - break - er, wher -

MOONGLOW

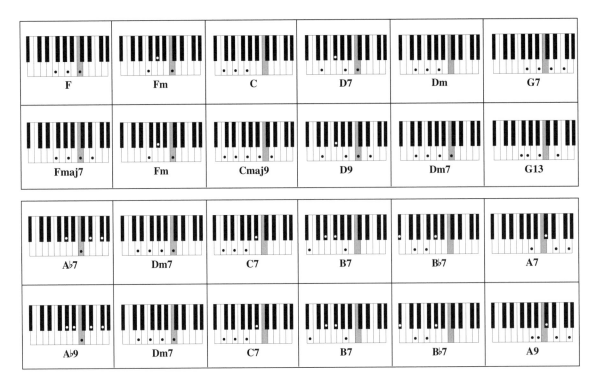

Copyright © 1934 Mills Music, Inc., New York
Copyright Renewed, Assigned to Mills Music, Inc.
and Scarsdale Music Corporation, New York for the United States
All Rights outside the United States Controlled by Mills Music, Inc.
International Copyright Secured   All Rights Reserved
Used by Permission

Words and Music by WILL HUDSON,
EDDIE DE LANGE and IRVING MILLS

It must have been moon-glow,   way up in the

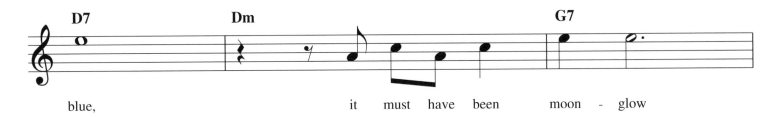

blue,   it must have been moon-glow

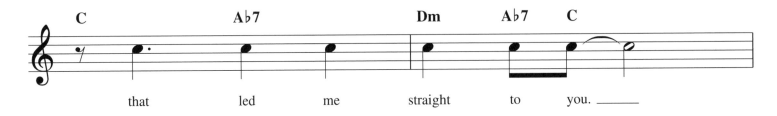

that   led   me   straight   to   you. _____

I still hear you say - ing,   "Dear one, hold me

MOONLIGHT IN VERMONT

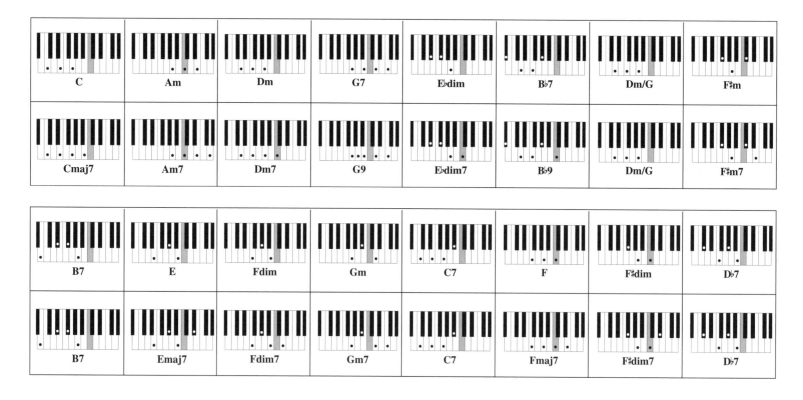

Copyright © 1944 (Renewed 1972) Michael H. Goldsen, Inc.
Copyright Renewed 2000 Michael H. Goldsen, Inc.
and Johnny R. Music Company in the U.S.
All Rights outside the U.S. Controlled by Michael H. Goldsen, Inc.
International Copyright Secured   All Rights Reserved

Words and Music by JOHN BLACKBURN
and KARL SUESSDORF

Pen - nies in a stream,

fall - ing leaves a sy - ca - more, moon - light in Ver -

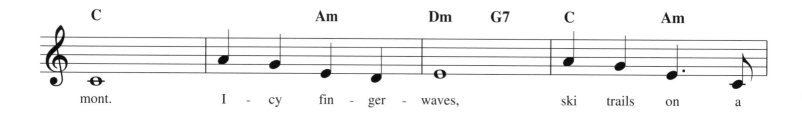

mont.   I - cy fin - ger - waves,   ski trails on a

MY FAVORITE THINGS
from THE SOUND OF MUSIC

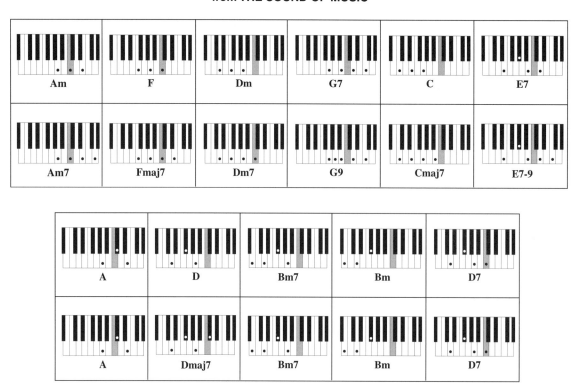

Copyright © 1959 by Richard Rodgers and Oscar Hammerstein II
Copyright Renewed
WILLIAMSON MUSIC owner of publication and allied rights throughout the world
International Copyright Secured   All Rights Reserved

Lyrics by OSCAR HAMMERSTEIN II
Music by RICHARD RODGERS

Rain - drops on ros - es and whis - kers on kit - tens,
Cream col - ored po - nies and crisp ap - ple strud - els,

bright cop - per ket - tles and warm wool - en mit - tens,
door - bells and sleigh - bells and schnitz - el with noo - dles,

brown pa - per pack - ag - es tied up with string,
wild geese that fly with the moon on their wings,

these are a few of my fa - vor - ite things.

MY FUNNY VALENTINE
from BABES IN ARMS

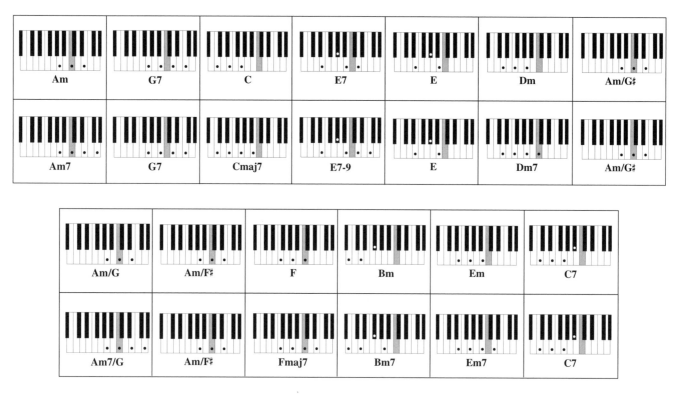

Copyright © 1937 (Renewed) by Chappell & Co.
Rights for the Extended Renewal Term in the U.S. Controlled by Williamson Music and
WB Music Corp. o/b/o The Estate Of Lorenz Hart
International Copyright Secured   All Rights Reserved

Words by LORENZ HART
Music by RICHARD RODGERS

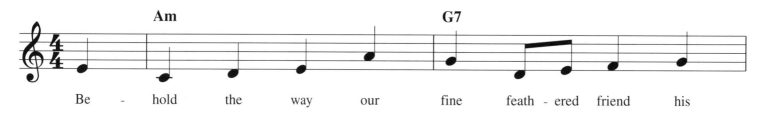

Be - hold the way our fine feath - ered friend his

vir - tue doth pa - rade. Thou know - est not my

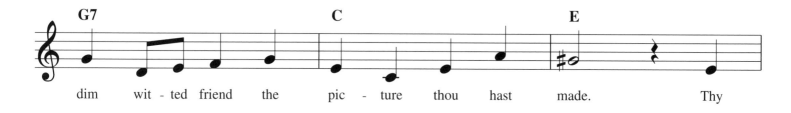

dim wit - ted friend the pic - ture thou hast made. Thy

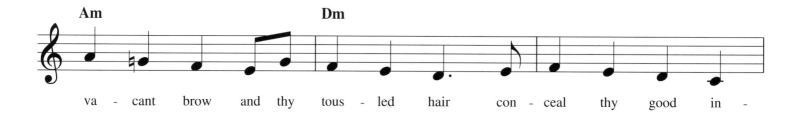

va - cant brow and thy tous - led hair con - ceal thy good in -

MY ROMANCE
from JUMBO

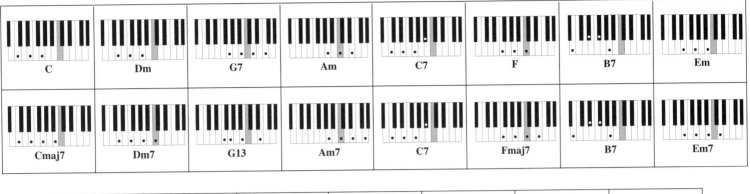

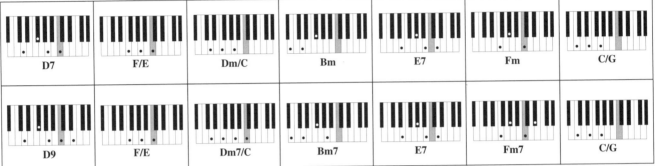

Copyright © 1935 by Williamson Music and Lorenz Hart Publishing Co.
Copyright Renewed
All Rights in the United States Administered by Williamson Music
All Rights outside of the United States Administered by Universal - PolyGram International Publishing, Inc.
International Copyright Secured   All Rights Reserved

Words by LORENZ HART
Music by RICHARD RODGERS

My ro-mance does-n't have to have a moon in the sky. My ro-mance does-n't need a blue la-goon stand-ing by; no month of May, no twin-kling stars, no hide-a-way, no soft gui-tars. My ro-

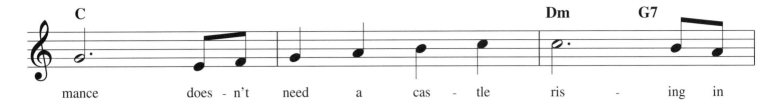

mance does-n't need a cas - tle ris - ing in

Spain, nor a dance in a con - stant - ly sur -

pris - ing re - frain. Wide a - wake I can

make my most fan - tas - tic dreams come true; my ro -

mance does-n't need a thing but you. _____

A NIGHTINGALE SANG IN BERKELEY SQUARE

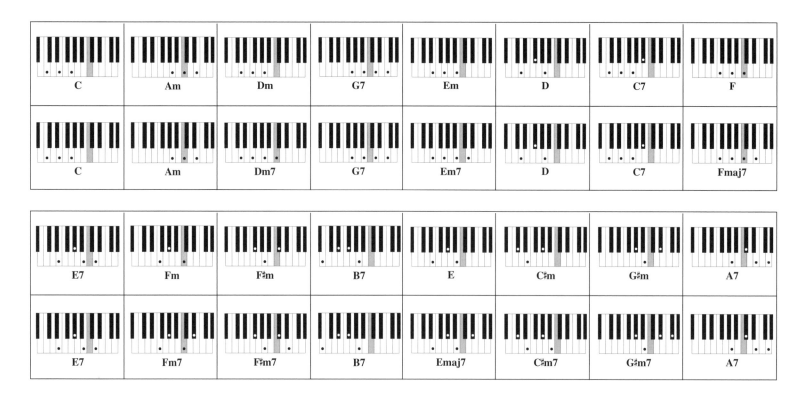

Copyright © 1940 The Peter Maurice Music Co., Ltd., London, England
Copyright Renewed and Assigned to Shapiro, Bernstein & Co., Inc., New York for U.S.A. and Canada
International Copyright Secured   All Rights Reserved
Used by Permission

Lyric by ERIC MASCHWITZ
Music by MANNING SHERWIN

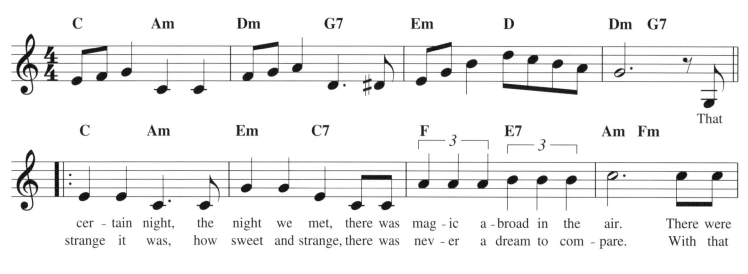

That

cer-tain night, the night we met, there was mag-ic a-broad in the air. There were
strange it was, how sweet and strange, there was nev-er a dream to com-pare. With that

an-gels din-ing at the Ritz, and a { night-in-gale sang in Berk-'ley
ha-zy, cra-zy night we met, when a {

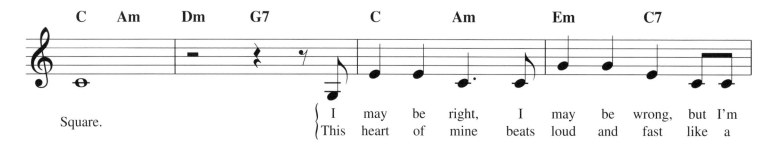

Square.

{ I may be right, I may be wrong, but I'm
{ This heart of mine beats loud and fast like a

RAINDROPS KEEP FALLIN' ON MY HEAD
from BUTCH CASSIDY AND THE SUNDANCE KID

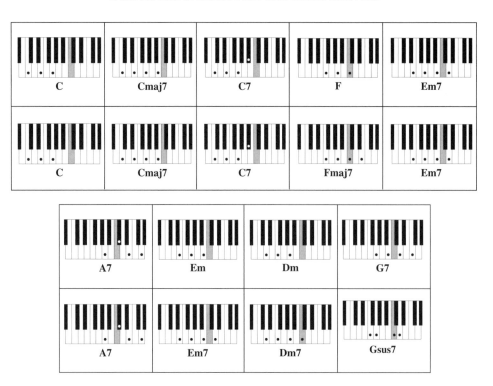

Copyright © 1969 (Renewed) Casa David, New Hidden Valley Music and WB Music Corp.
International Copyright Secured   All Rights Reserved

Lyric by HAL DAVID
Music by BURT BACHARACH

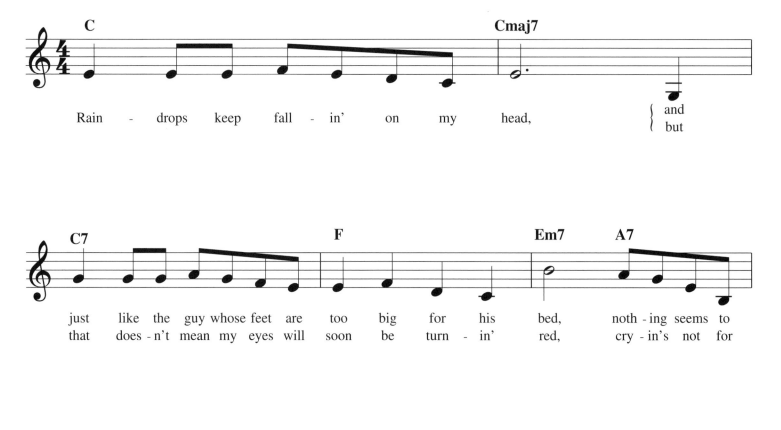

Rain - drops keep fall - in' on my head, and / but

just like the guy whose feet are too big for his bed, noth - ing seems to
that does - n't mean my eyes will soon be turn - in' red, cry - in's not for

fit. Those rain - drops keep fall - in' on my head, they keep fall - in'.
me. 'Cause I'm nev - er gon - na stop the rain by com - plain - in'

RIBBON IN THE SKY

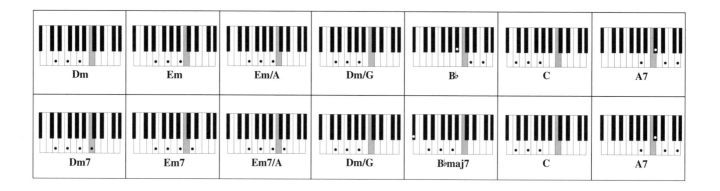

© 1982 JOBETE MUSIC CO., INC. and BLACK BULL MUSIC
c/o EMI APRIL MUSIC INC.
All Rights Reserved   International Copyright Secured   Used by Permission

Words and Music by
STEVIE WONDER

(Instrumental)

1. Oh, so long for this night I prayed __ that a
2. lowed may I touch your hand, __ and if
3.,4.*(See additional lyrics)*

star would guide you my way _____ to share
pleased may I once a - gain, _____ so that

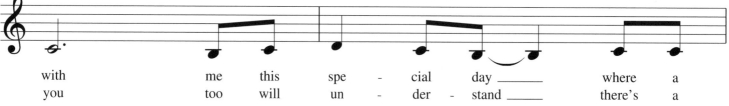

with me this spe - cial day _____ where a
you too will un - der - stand _____ there's a

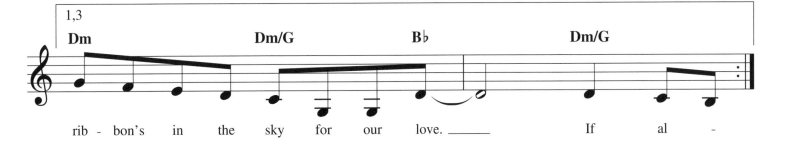

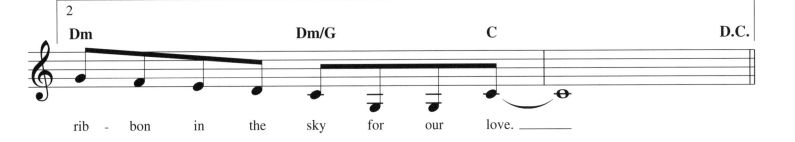

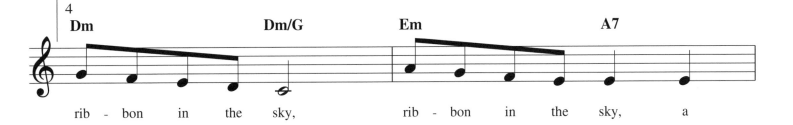

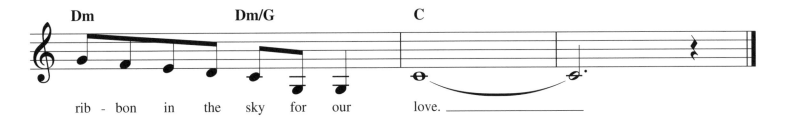

Additional Lyrics

3. This is not a coincidence,
   And far more than a lucky chance.
   But what is that is always meant
   Is our ribbon in the sky for our love.

4. We can't lose with God on our side.
   From now on it will be you and I
   And our ribbon in the sky, ribbon in the sky,
   A ribbon in the sky for our love.

SATIN DOLL
from SOPHISTICATED LADIES

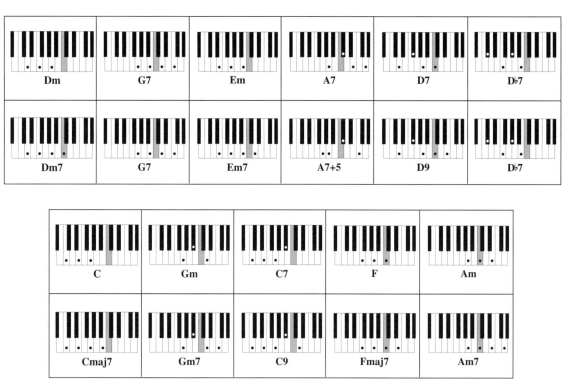

Copyright © 1958 (Renewed 1986) and Assigned to Famous Music LLC
WB Music Corp. and Tempo Music, Inc. c/o Music Sales Corporation in the U.S.A.
Rights for the world outside the U.S.A. Controlled by Tempo Music, Inc.
c/o Music Sales Corporation
International Copyright Secured   All Rights Reserved

Words by JOHNNY MERCER and BILLY STRAYHORN
Music by DUKE ELLINGTON

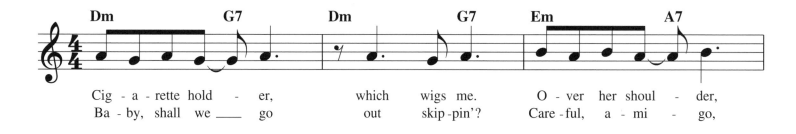

Cig - a - rette hold - er,   which   wigs me.   O - ver her shoul - der,
Ba - by, shall we ___ go   out   skip -pin'?   Care -ful, a - mi - go,

she   digs   me   Out   cat - tin'   that   sat - in
you're   flip - pin'.   Speaks   Lat - in,   that   sat - in

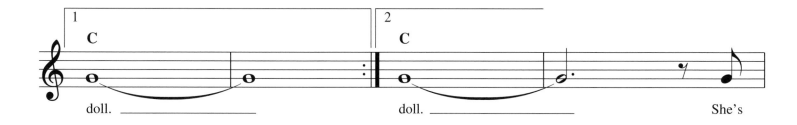

doll. ___   doll. ___   She's

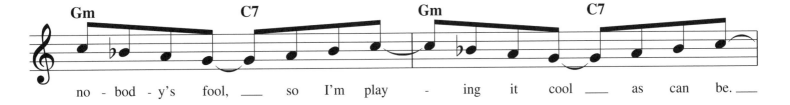

no - bod - y's fool, ___ so I'm play - ing it cool ___ as can be. ___

___ I'll give it a whirl, ___ but I ain't ___

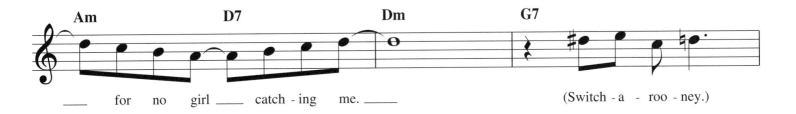

___ for no girl ___ catch - ing me. ___ (Switch - a - roo - ney.)

Tel - e - phone num - bers; well, you know,

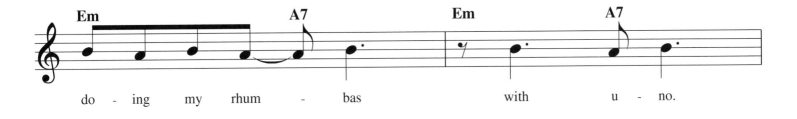

do - ing my rhum - bas with u - no.

And that 'n' my sat - in doll. ___

SAVING ALL MY LOVE FOR YOU

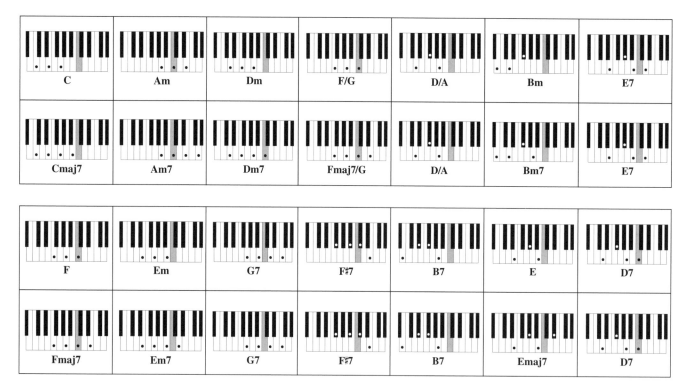

© 1978 SCREEN GEMS-EMI MUSIC INC., LAUREN-WESLEY MUSIC INC. and PRINCE STREET MUSIC
All Rights for LAUREN-WESLEY MUSIC INC. Controlled and Administered by SCREEN GEMS-EMI MUSIC INC.
All Rights Reserved   International Copyright Secured   Used by Permission

Words by GERRY GOFFIN
Music by MICHAEL MASSER

A few _____ sto - len mo - ments _____ is all _____ that we
not _____ ver - y eas - y _____ liv - ing all a -
got _____ to get read - y, _____ just a few _____ min - utes

share. You've _____ got your fam - 'ly and
lone. My friends _____ try and tell me _____ find a
more. Gon - na get _____ that old feel - ing _____ when you

they _____ need you there. _____ Though I try _____ to re -
man of my own. _____ But each _____ time I
walk _____ through that door. _____ 'Cause to - night _____ is the

sist _____ be - ing last _____ on your list, _____ but
try, _____ I just break _____ down and cry. 'Cause I'd
night _____ for feel - ing all right. We'll be

no oth - er man's _____ gon - na do. _____
rath - er be home _____ feel - in' blue. _____
mak _ ing love the whole _____ night ___ through. _____

To Coda ⊕

_____ } So I'm sav - ing all my love for you. ___

(Instrumental) _____ It's

(Instrumental) _____ You used to

tell me _____ we'd run a - way to - geth - er; _____

love gives you the right _____ to be free. _____

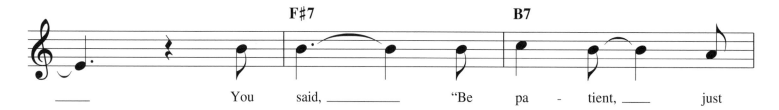

You said, _____ "Be pa - tient, _____ just

wait a lit - tle long - er," _____ but that's just _____ an

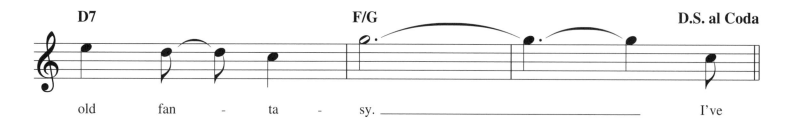

old fan - ta - sy. _____ I've

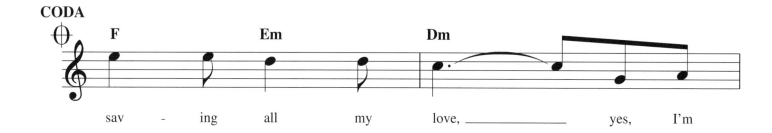

CODA

sav - ing all my love, _____ yes, I'm

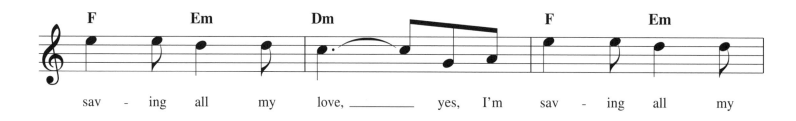

sav - ing all my love, _____ yes, I'm sav - ing all my

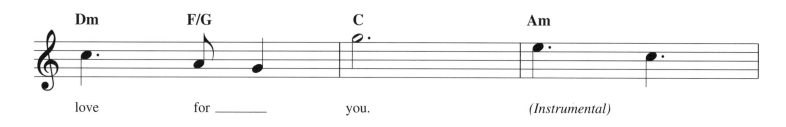

love for _____ you. *(Instrumental)*

No oth - er

wom - an _____ is gon - na love you more, ____

_____ 'cause to - night _____ is the night _____ that I'm

feel - ing all right. _____ We'll be

mak - ing love the whole _____ night ____ through. _____

_____ So I'm sav - ing all my love, yes, I'm

sav - ing all my lov - ing, _____ yes, I'm

sav - ing all my love for you. _____

SENTIMENTAL JOURNEY

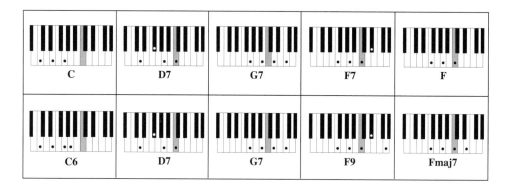

© 1944 (Renewed) MORLEY MUSIC CO. and HOLLIDAY PUBLISHING
All Rights Reserved

Words and Music by BUD GREEN,
LES BROWN and BEN HOMER

SKYLARK

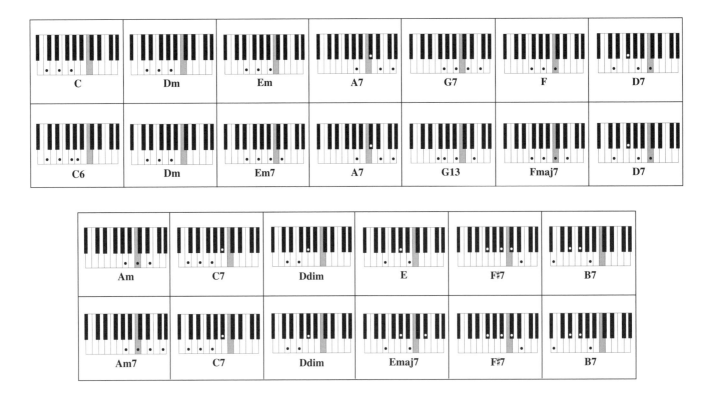

Copyright © 1941, 1942 by Songs Of Peer, Ltd. and WB Music Corp.
Copyright Renewed
International Copyright Secured   All Rights Reserved

Words by JOHNNY MERCER
Music by HOAGY CARMICHAEL

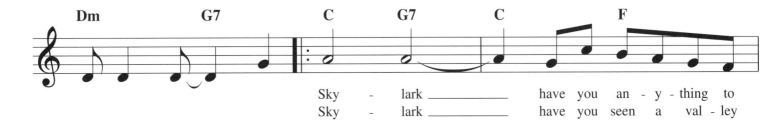

Sky - lark _____ have you an - y - thing to
Sky - lark _____ have you seen a val - ley

say to me? _____ Won't you tell me where my love can be? _____
green with spring? _____ Where my heart can go a jour - ney - ing? _____

_____ Is there a mead - ow in the mist, _____ where some - one's wait - ing to be kissed?
_____ O - ver the shad - ows and the

SMOKE GETS IN YOUR EYES
from ROBERTA

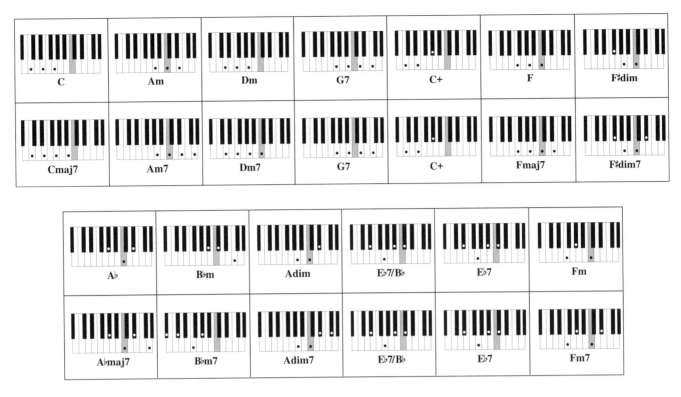

Copyright © 1933 UNIVERSAL - POLYGRAM INTERNATIONAL PUBLISHING, INC.
Copyright Renewed
All Rights Reserved   Used by Permission

Words by OTTO HARBACH
Music by JEROME KERN

So I chaffed _____ them and I gay - ly laughed _____ to think they could

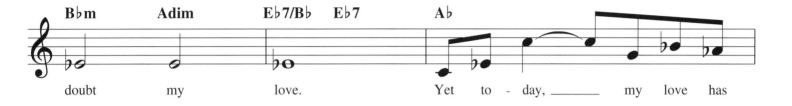

doubt my love. Yet to - day, _____ my love has

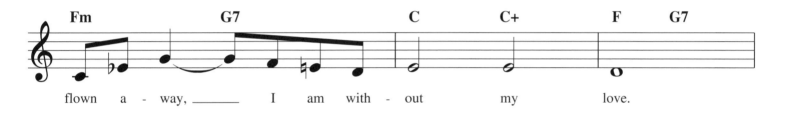

flown a - way, _____ I am with - out my love.

Now laugh - ing friends de - ride, tears I can - not

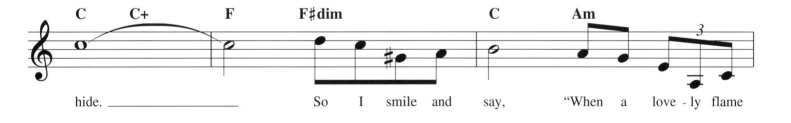

hide. _____ So I smile and say, "When a love - ly flame

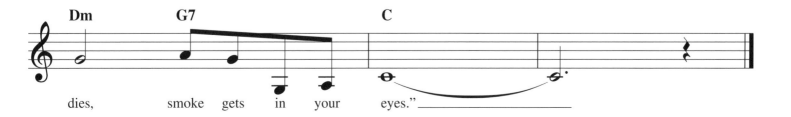

dies, smoke gets in your eyes." _____

SOLITUDE

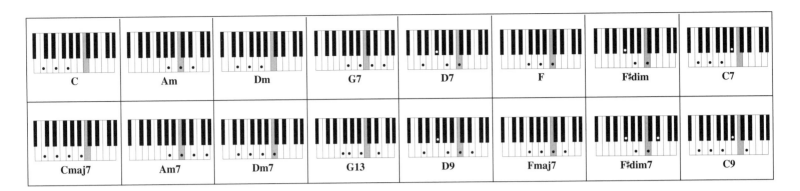

Copyright © 1934 (Renewed 1961) and Assigned to Famous Music LLC,
Scarsdale Music Corp. and EMI Mills Music Inc. in the U.S.A.
Rights for the world outside the U.S.A. Controlled by EMI Mills Music Inc. (Publishing) and Warner Bros. Publications U.S. Inc. (Print)
International Copyright Secured   All Rights Reserved

Words and Music by DUKE ELLINGTON,
EDDIE DE LANGE and IRVING MILLS

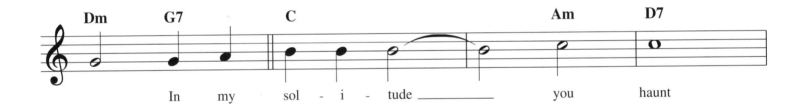

In my sol - i - tude _____ you haunt

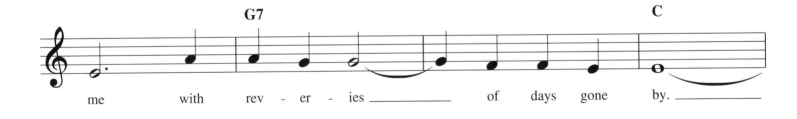

me with rev - er - ies _____ of days gone by. _____

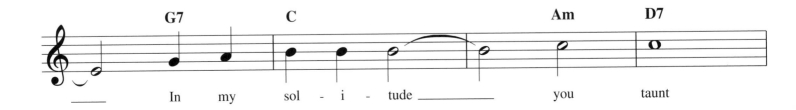

_____ In my sol - i - tude _____ you taunt

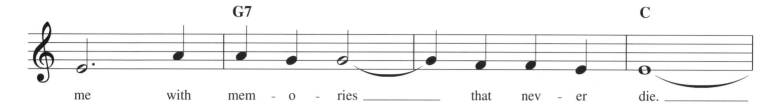

me with mem - o - ries _____ that nev - er die. _____

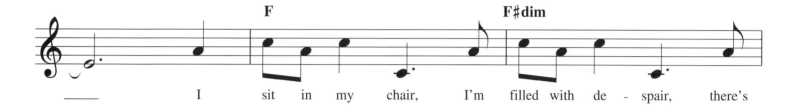

_____ I sit in my chair, I'm filled with de - spair, there's

no one could be so sad. With gloom ev - 'ry - where, I

sit and I stare. I know that I'll soon go mad. In my

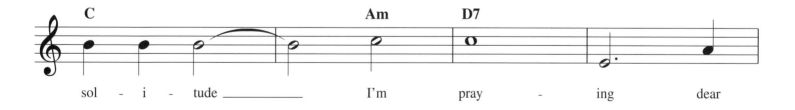

sol - i - tude _____ I'm pray - ing dear

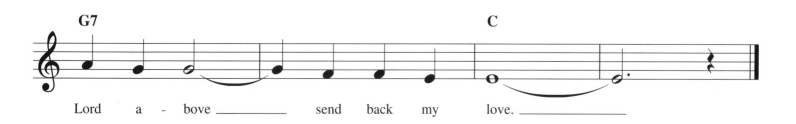

Lord a - bove _____ send back my love. _____

SOMEWHERE OUT THERE
from AN AMERICAN TAIL

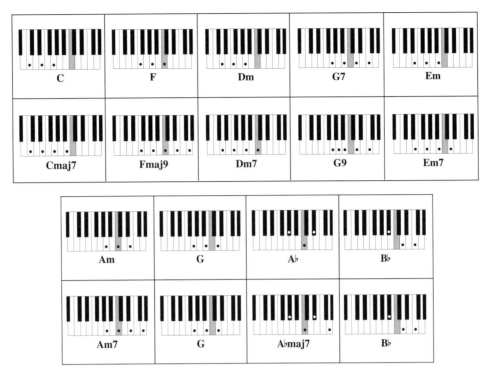

Copyright © 1986 USI A MUSIC PUBLISHING and USI B MUSIC PUBLISHING
All Rights Controlled and Administered by UNIVERSAL MUSIC CORP.
and SONGS OF UNIVERSAL, INC.
All Rights Reserved   Used by Permission

Music by BARRY MANN and JAMES HORNER
Lyric by CYNTHIA WEIL

F   G   F   G

e - ven though I know how ver - y   far a - part we are,   it

F   G   F   G

helps to think we might be wish - in'   on the same bright star.   And

A♭   B♭   A♭   B♭

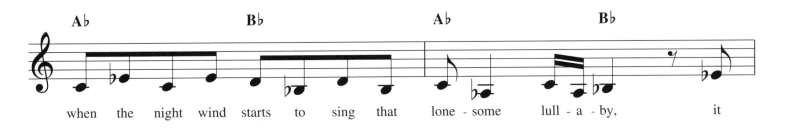

when the night wind starts to sing that   lone - some lull - a - by,   it

A♭   B♭   G   **D.C. al Coda**

helps to think we're sleep - ing un - der - neath the same big sky.

CODA

Em   Am   F   G   C

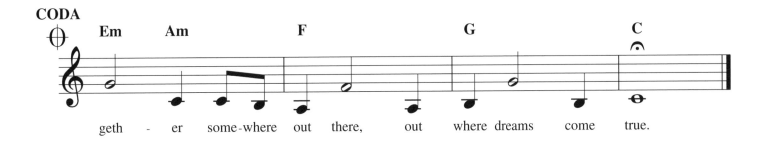

geth - er some-where out there,   out where dreams come true.

SOPHISTICATED LADY
from SOPHISTICATED LADIES

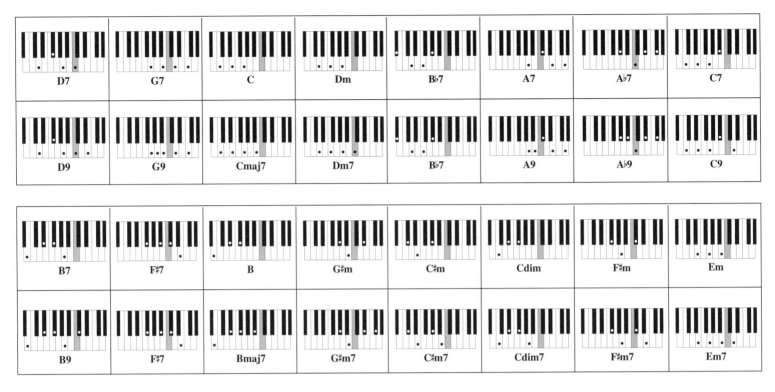

Copyright © 1933 (Renewed 1960) and Assigned to Famous Music LLC
and EMI Mills Music Inc. in the U.S.A.
Rights for the world outside the U.S.A. Controlled by EMI Mills Music Inc. (Publishing)
and Warner Bros. Publications U.S. Inc. (Print)
International Copyright Secured   All Rights Reserved

Words and Music by DUKE ELLINGTON,
IRVING MILLS and MITCHELL PARISH

STAND BY ME

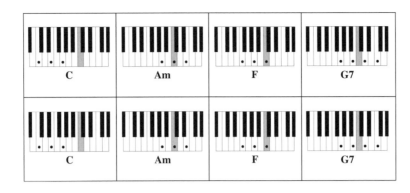

© 1961 (Renewed) JERRY LEIBER MUSIC, MIKE STOLLER MUSIC and MIKE & JERRY MUSIC LLC
All Rights Reserved

Words and Music by JERRY LEIBER,
MIKE STOLLER and BEN E. KING

When the night _____ has come and the land is dark and the moon _____ is the on-ly _____ light we'll see. No, I won't be a-fraid, no _____ I _____ won't be a-fraid just as long _____ as you stand, _____ stand by me. So, dar-ling, dar-ling, stand _____ by me, oh, _____

Am … **F** … **G7**

stand _____ by me, oh, stand, _____ stand by me,

C … **Fine** … **C** … *3*

stand by me. _____ If the sea _____ that we look up - on

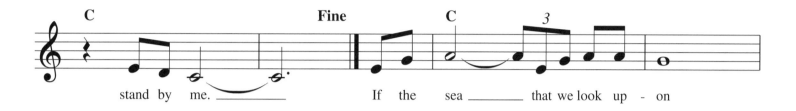

Am … **F**

should tum - ble and fall, or the moun - tain _____ should

G7 … **C**

crum - ble _____ in the sea, I won't cry, I won't

Am

cry, no _____ I _____ won't shed a tear just as

F … **G7** … **C** … **D.S. al Fine**

long _____ as you stand, _____ stand by me. So, dar - ling, dar - ling,

STARDUST

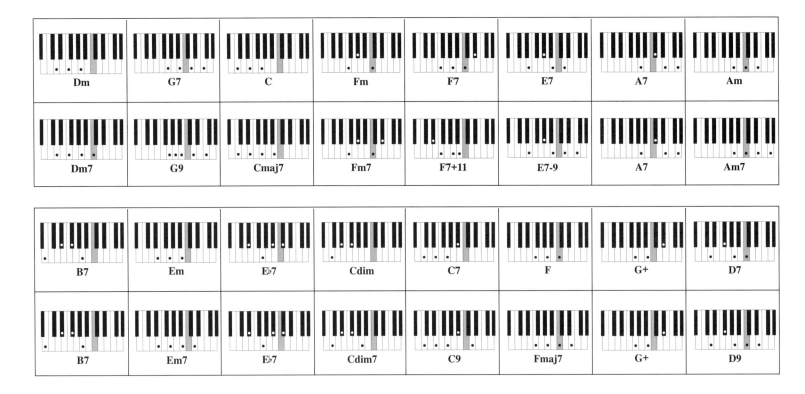

Copyright © 1928, 1929 by Songs Of Peer, Ltd. and EMI Mills Music, Inc.
Copyrights Renewed
All Rights outside the USA Controlled by EMI Mills Music, Inc. (Publishing)
    and Warner Bros. Publications U.S. Inc. (Print)
International Copyright Secured   All Rights Reserved

Words by MITCHELL PARISH
Music by HOAGY CARMICHAEL

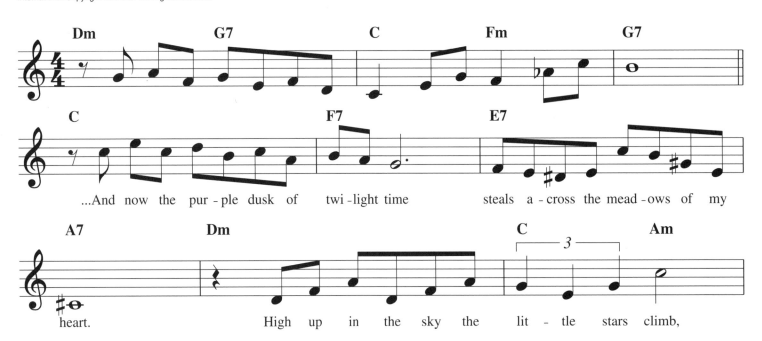

...And now the pur-ple dusk of twi-light time steals a-cross the mead-ows of my heart. High up in the sky the lit-tle stars climb, al-ways re-mind-ing me that we're a-part. You wan-dered down the lane and far a-way, leav-ing me a song that will not die.

STELLA BY STARLIGHT
from the Paramount Picture THE UNINVITED

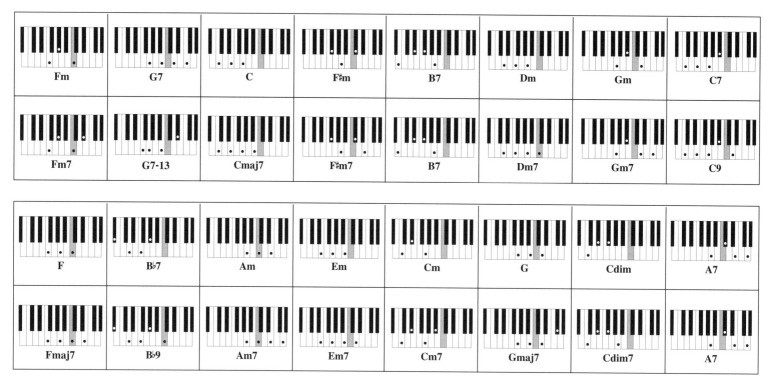

Copyright © 1946 (Renewed 1973, 1974) by Famous Music LLC
International Copyright Secured   All Rights Reserved

Words by NED WASHINGTON
Music by VICTOR YOUNG

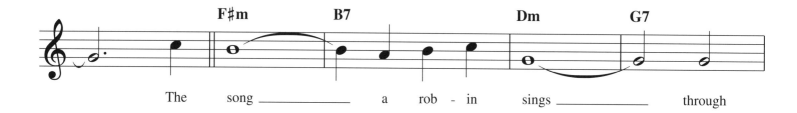

The song _____ a rob-in sings _____ through

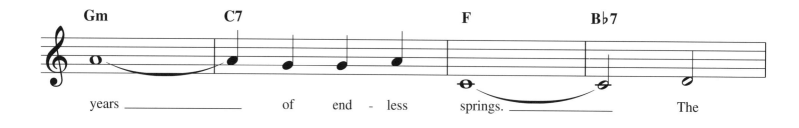

years _____ of end-less springs. _____ The

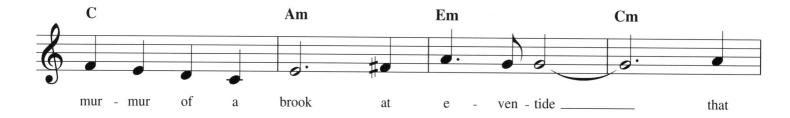

mur-mur of a brook at e-ven-tide _____ that

STORMY WEATHER
(Keeps Rainin' All the Time)
from COTTON CLUB PARADE OF 1933

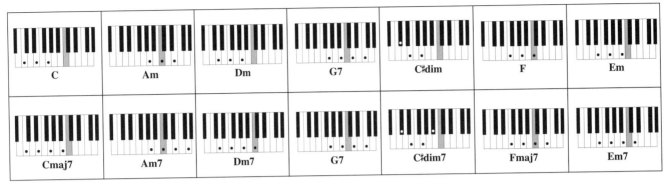

© 1933 (Renewed 1961) TED KOEHLER MUSIC and S.A. MUSIC CO.
All Rights for TED KOEHLER MUSIC Administered by
 FRED AHLERT MUSIC CORPORATION
All Rights Reserved

Lyric by TED KOEHLER
Music by HAROLD ARLEN

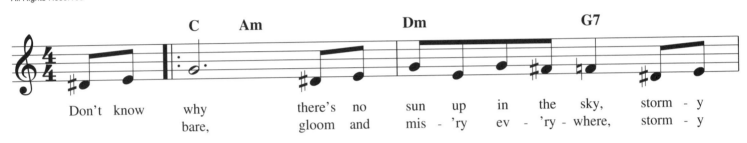

Don't know why there's no sun up in the sky, storm-y
bare, gloom and mis - 'ry ev - 'ry - where, storm-y

weath - er. Since my man and I ain't to - geth - er, _____
weath - er. Just can't get my poor self to - geth - er. _____

keeps rain - in' all the time. _____ Life is
So wear - y all the

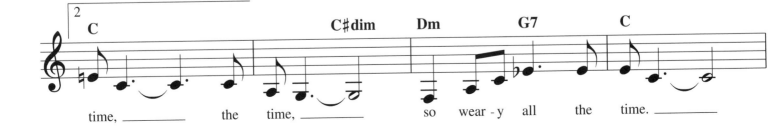

time, _____ the time, _____ so wear - y all the time. _____

TANGERINE
from the Paramount Picture THE FLEET'S IN

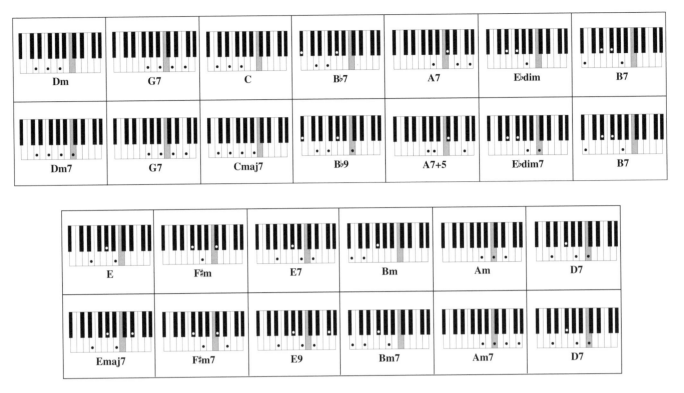

Copyright © 1942 (Renewed 1969) by Famous Music LLC
International Copyright Secured   All Rights Reserved

Words by JOHNNY MERCER
Music by VICTOR SCHERTZINGER

Tan - ger -

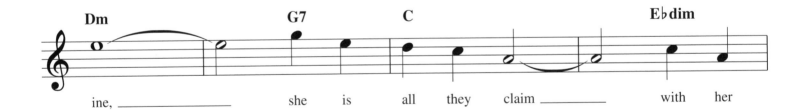

ine, _____ she is all they claim _____ with her

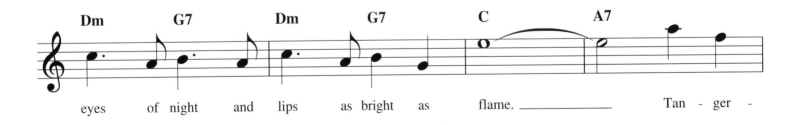

eyes of night and lips as bright as flame. _____ Tan - ger -

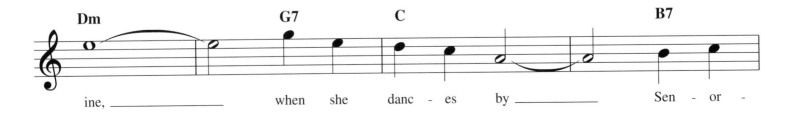

ine, _____ when she danc - es by _____ Sen - or -

i - tas stare and ca - bal - le - ros sigh. _____ And I've

seen _____ toasts to Tan - ger - ine _____ raised in

ev - 'ry bar a - cross the Ar - gen - tine. _____ Yes, she

has them all on the run but her heart be - longs to just one. Her

heart be - longs to Tan - ger - ine. _____

TEARS IN HEAVEN

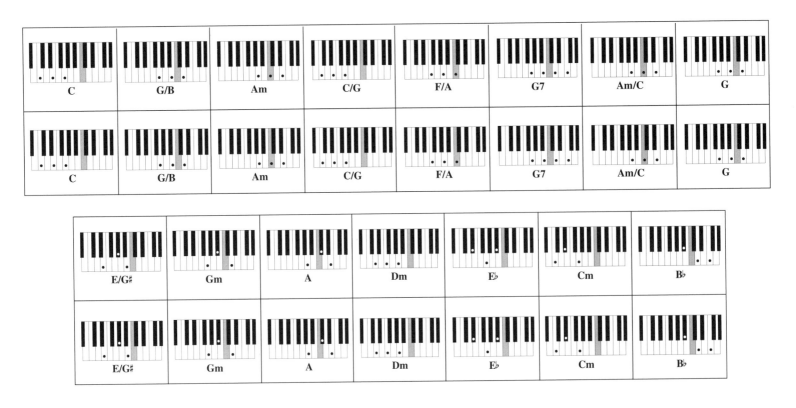

Copyright © 1992 by E.C. Music Ltd. and Blue Sky Rider Songs
All Rights for E.C. Music Ltd. Administered by Unichappell Music Inc.
All Rights for Blue Sky Rider Songs Administered by Irving Music, Inc.
International Copyright Secured   All Rights Reserved

Words and Music by ERIC CLAPTON
and WILL JENNINGS

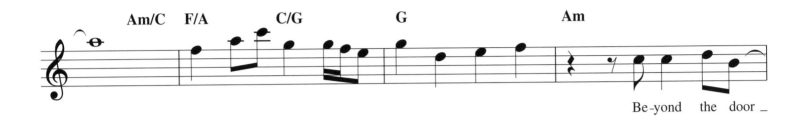

Be-yond the door _

_ there's peace, I'm sure, ___ and I know _

_ there'll be no more ___ tears in heav - en. *(Instrumental)*

CODA

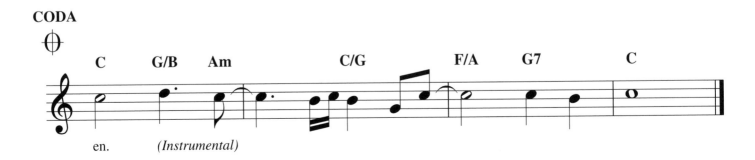

en. *(Instrumental)*

TWIST AND SHOUT

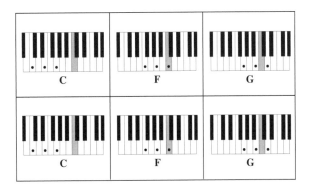

Copyright © 1964 Sony/ATV Songs LLC and Sloopy II Music
Copyright Renewed
All Rights on behalf of Sony/ATV Songs LLC Administered by Sony/ATV Music Publishing,
8 Music Square West, Nashville, TN 37203
International Copyright Secured   All Rights Reserved

Words and Music by BERT RUSSELL
and PHIL MEDLEY

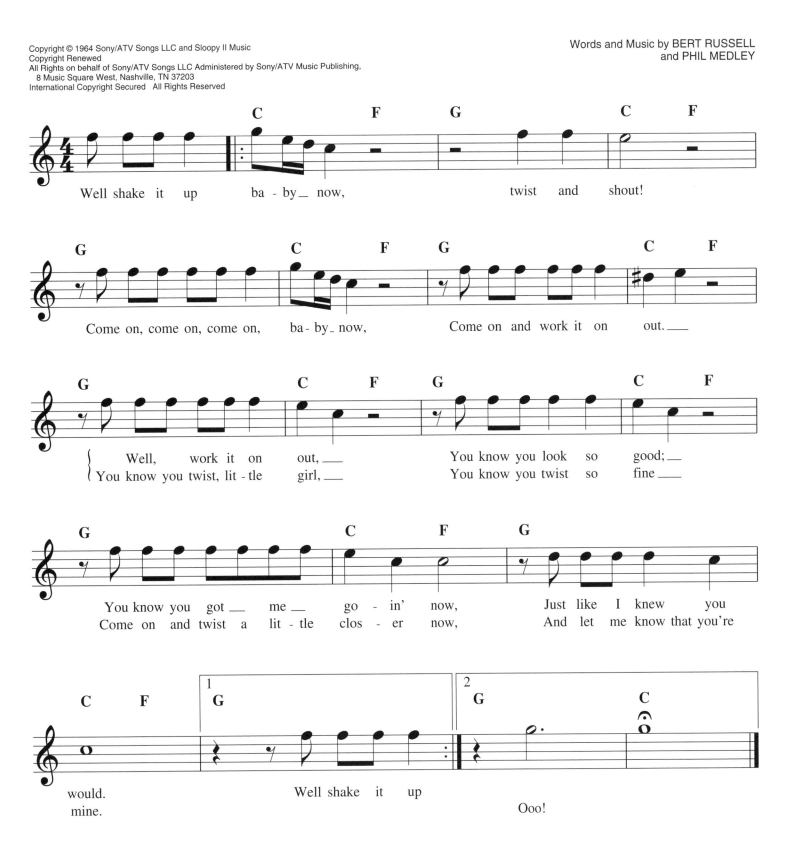

TILL THERE WAS YOU
from Meredith Willson's THE MUSIC MAN

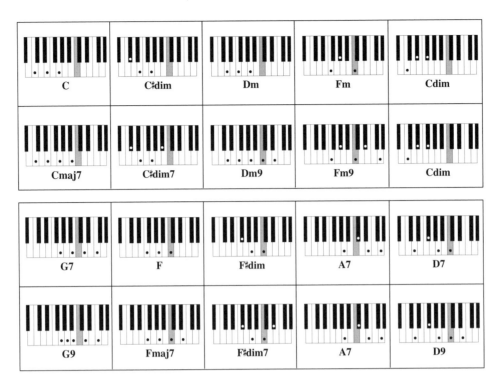

© 1950, 1957 (Renewed) FRANK MUSIC CORP. and MEREDITH WILLSON MUSIC
All Rights Reserved

By MEREDITH WILLSON

There were bells on the hill, but I
birds in the sky, but I

nev - er heard them ring - ing. No, I nev - er heard them at
nev - er saw them wing - ing. No, I nev - er saw them at

all, till there was you.
all, till there was

you. There were

you. And there was mu - sic and

TRY TO REMEMBER

from THE FANTASTICS

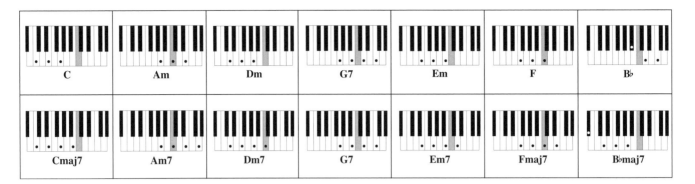

Copyright © 1960 by Tom Jones and Harvey Schmidt
Copyright Renewed
Chappell & Co. owner of publication and allied rights throughout the world
International Copyright Secured   All Rights Reserved

Words by TOM JONES
Music by HARVEY SCHMIDT

WALTZ FOR DEBBY

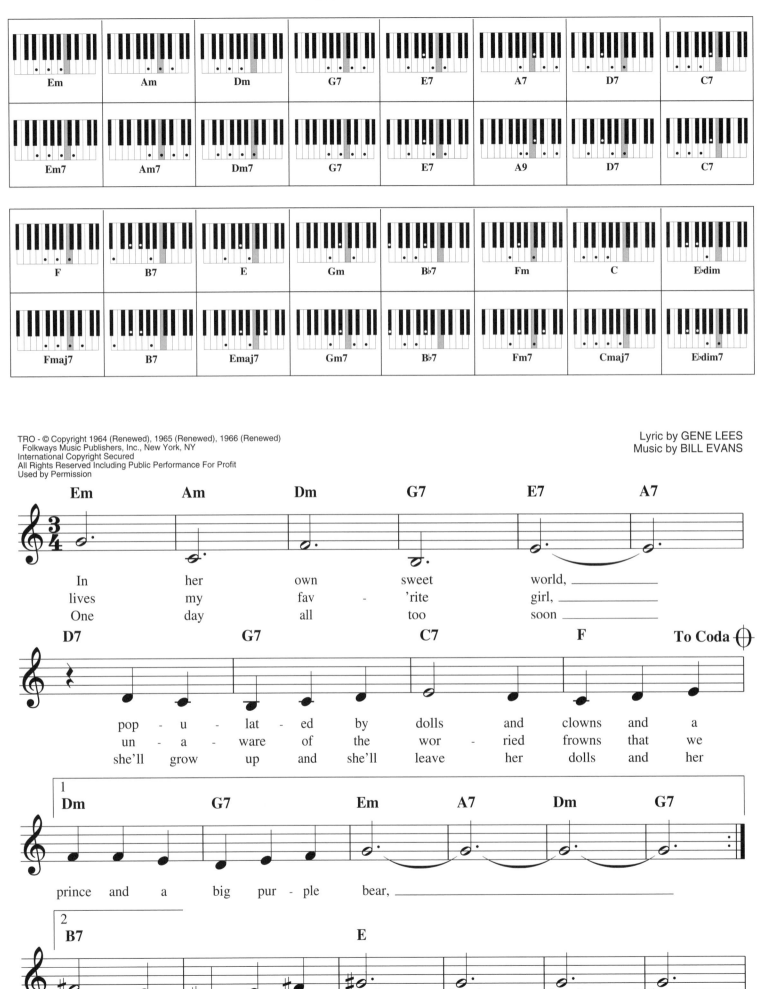

TRO - © Copyright 1964 (Renewed), 1965 (Renewed), 1966 (Renewed)
Folkways Music Publishers, Inc., New York, NY
International Copyright Secured
All Rights Reserved Including Public Performance For Profit
Used by Permission

Lyric by GENE LEES
Music by BILL EVANS

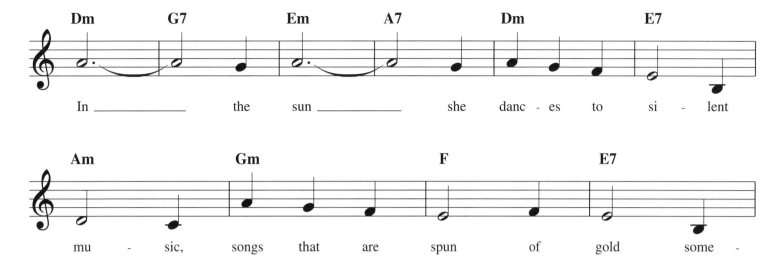

In _____ the sun _____ she danc - es to si - lent

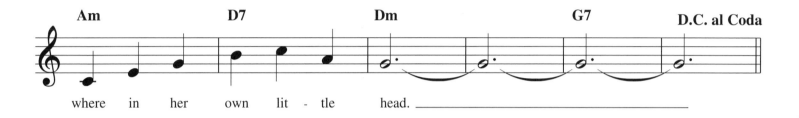

mu - sic, songs that are spun of gold some -

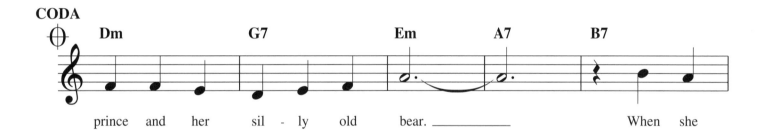

where in her own lit - tle head. _____

CODA

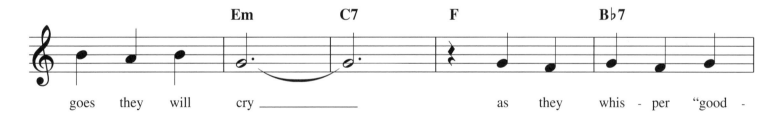

prince and her sil - ly old bear. _____ When she

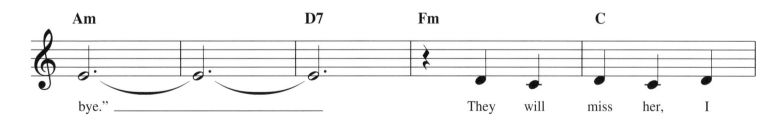

goes they will cry _____ as they whis - per "good -

bye." _____ They will miss her, I

fear, but, then, so will I. _____

THE WAY WE WERE
from the Motion Picture THE WAY WE WERE

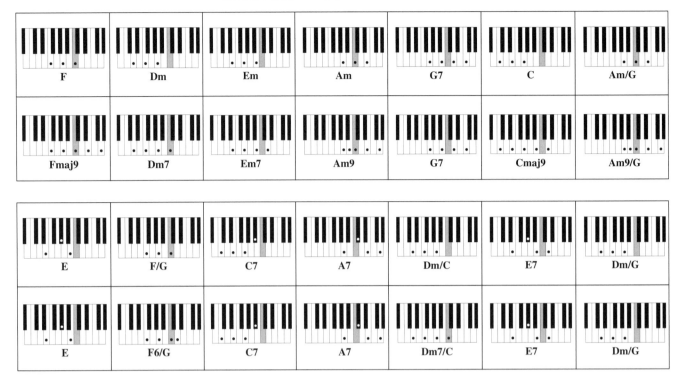

© 1973 (Renewed 2001) COLGEMS-EMI MUSIC INC.
All Rights Reserved   International Copyright Secured   Used by Permission

Words by ALAN and MARILYN BERGMAN
Music by MARVIN HAMLISCH

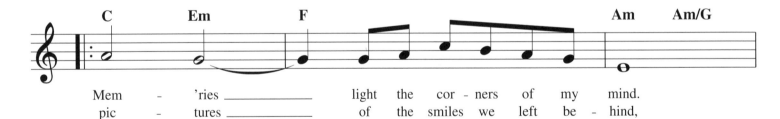

Mem - 'ries _____ light the cor - ners of my mind.
pic - tures _____ of the smiles we left be - hind,

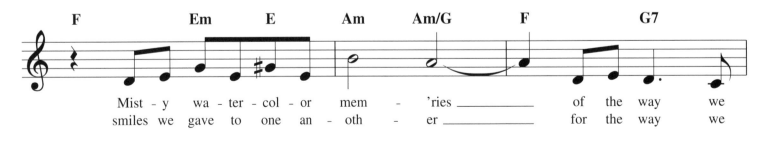

Mist - y wa - ter - col - or mem - 'ries _____ of the way we
smiles we gave to one an - oth - er _____ for the way we

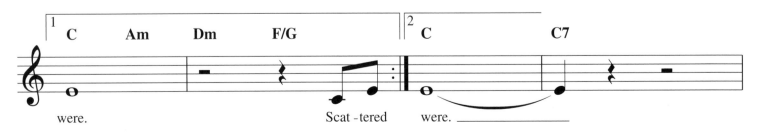

were.
Scat - tered

were. _____

THE WAY YOU LOOK TONIGHT
from SWING TIME

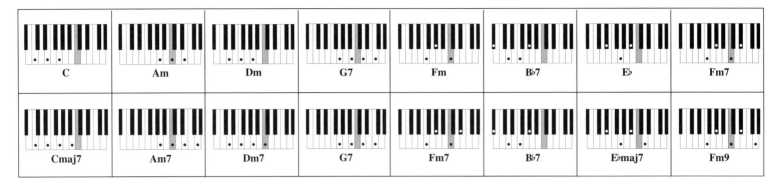

Copyright © 1936 UNIVERSAL - POLYGRAM INTERNATIONAL PUBLISHING, INC. and ALDI MUSIC
Copyright Renewed
Print Rights for ALDI MUSIC in the U.S. Controlled and Administered by
    HAPPY ASPEN MUSIC LLC c/o SHAPIRO, BERNSTEIN & CO., INC.
All Rights Reserved   Used by Permission

Words by DOROTHY FIELDS
Music by JEROME KERN

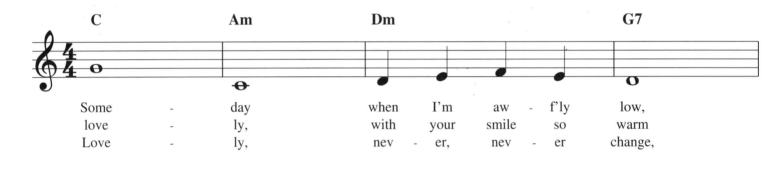

Some - day, when I'm aw - f'ly low,
love - ly, with your smile so warm
Love - ly, nev - er, nev - er change,

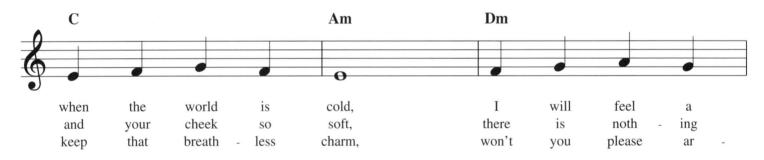

when the world is cold, I will feel a
and your cheek is so soft, there is noth - ing
keep that breath - less charm, won't you please ar -

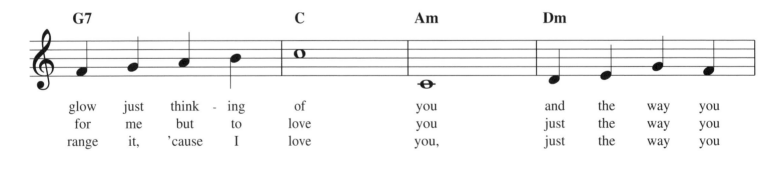

glow just think - ing of you and the way you
for me but to love you just the way you
range it, 'cause I love you, just the way you

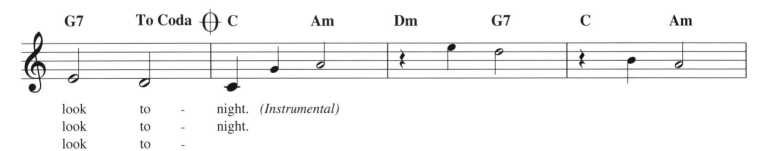

look to - night. (Instrumental)
look to - night.
look to -

Oh, but you're ... With each word your

ten - der - ness grows, _____ tear - ing my fear _____ a -

part, _____ and that laugh that

wrin - kles your nose _____ touch - es my fool - ish

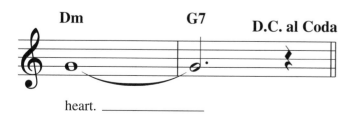

heart. _____

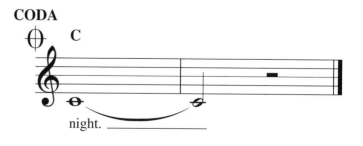

night. _____

WHAT A WONDERFUL WORLD

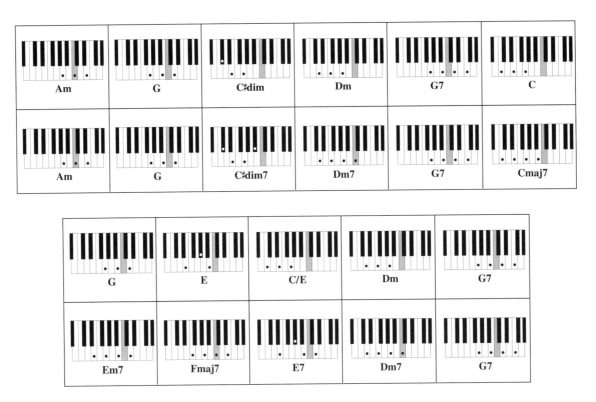

Copyright © 1967 by Range Road Music Inc., Quartet Music and Abilene Music, Inc.
Copyright Renewed
International Copyright Secured   All Rights Reserved
Used by Permission

Words and Music by GEORGE DAVID WEISS
and BOB THIELE

WHEN I FALL IN LOVE
from ONE MINUTE TO ZERO

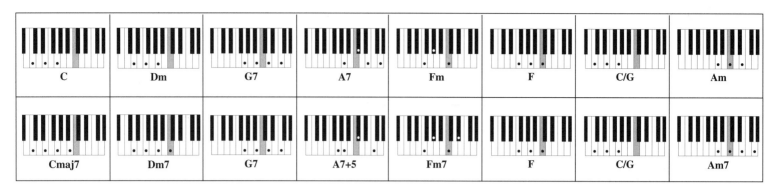

Copyright © 1952 by Chappell & Co. and Intersong U.S.A., Inc.
Copyright Renewed
International Copyright Secured All Rights Reserved

Words by EDWARD HEYMAN
Music by VICTOR YOUNG

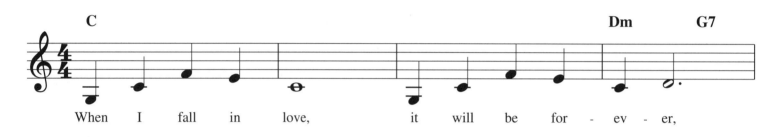

When I fall in love, it will be for - ev - er,

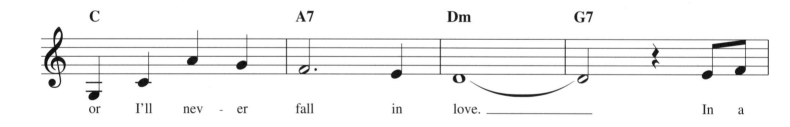

or I'll nev - er fall in love. _____ In a

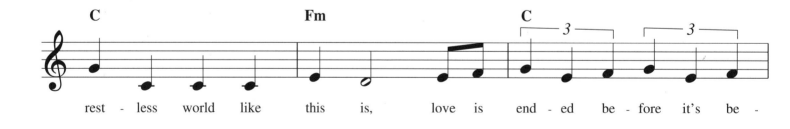

rest - less world like this is, love is end - ed be - fore it's be -

gun. And too man - y moon - light kiss - es seem to

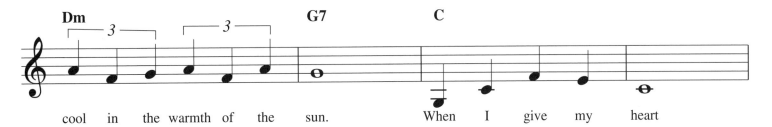

cool in the warmth of the sun. When I give my heart

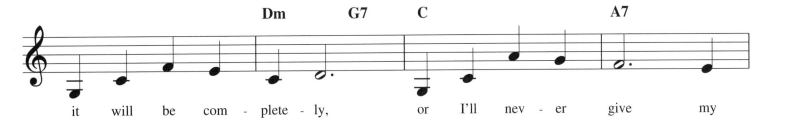

it will be com - plete - ly, or I'll nev - er give my

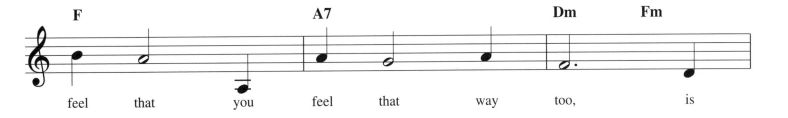

heart. _____ And the mo - ment I can

feel that you feel that way too, is

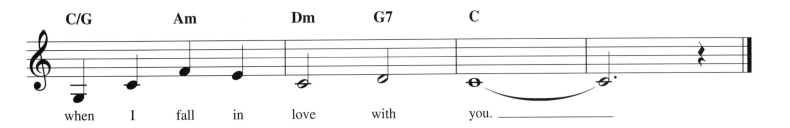

when I fall in love with you. _____

WHEN THE SAINTS GO MARCHING IN

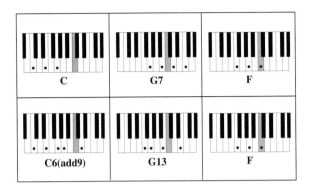

Copyright © 1997 by HAL LEONARD CORPORATION
International Copyright Secured   All Rights Reserved

Words by KATHERINE E. PURVIS
Music by JAMES M. BLACK

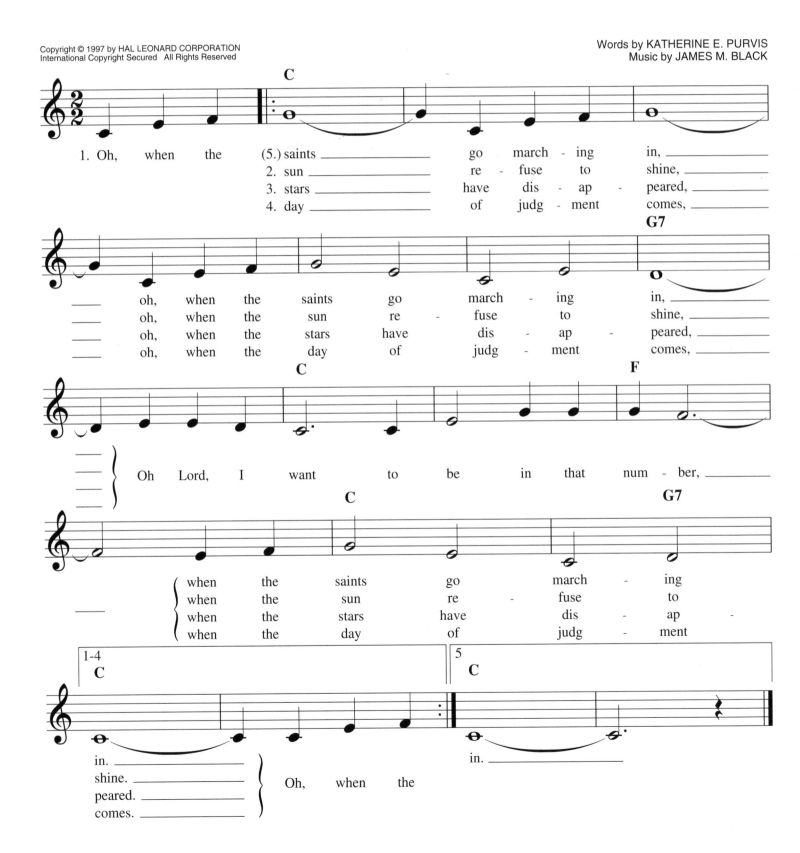

YESTERDAY

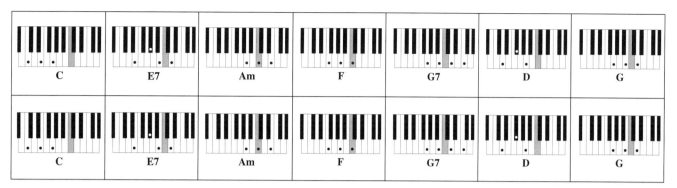

Copyright © 1965 Sony/ATV Songs LLC
Copyright Renewed
All Rights Administered by Sony/ATV Music Publishing, 8 Music Square West, Nashville, TN 37203
International Copyright Secured   All Rights Reserved

Words and Music by JOHN LENNON
and PAUL McCARTNEY

WONDERFUL TONIGHT

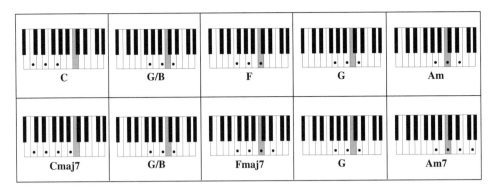

Copyright © 1977 by Eric Patrick Clapton
Copyright Renewed
All Rights for the U.S. Administered by Unichappell Music Inc.
International Copyright Secured   All Rights Reserved

Words and Music by
ERIC CLAPTON

YOUR CHEATIN' HEART

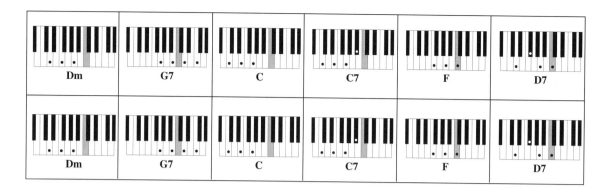

Copyright © 1952 Sony/ATV Songs LLC and Hiriam Music in the U.S.A.
Copyright Renewed
All Rights on behalf of Hiriam Music Administered by Rightsong Music Inc.
All Rights outside the U.S.A. Controlled by Sony/ATV Songs LLC
All Rights on behalf of Sony/ATV Songs LLC Administered by Sony/ATV Music Publishing, 8 Music Square West, Nashville, TN 37203
International Copyright Secured   All Rights Reserved

Words and Music by
HANK WILLIAMS

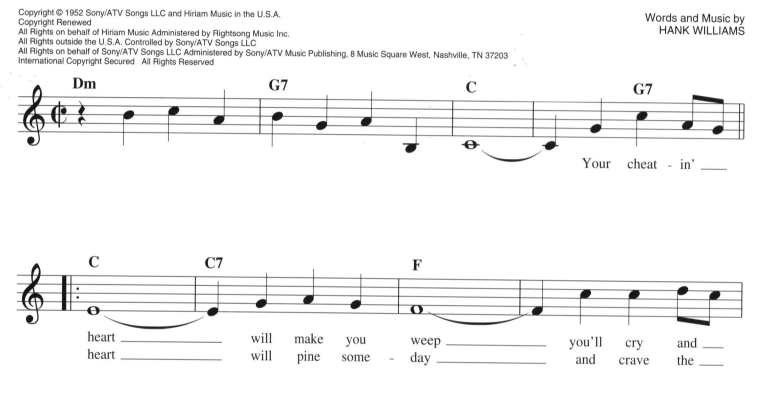

Your cheat - in' ____

heart _____ will make you weep _____ you'll cry and ____
heart _____ will pine some - day _____ and crave the ____

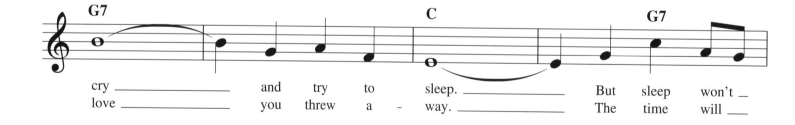

cry _____ and try to sleep. _____ But sleep won't ____
love _____ you threw a - way. _____ The time will ____

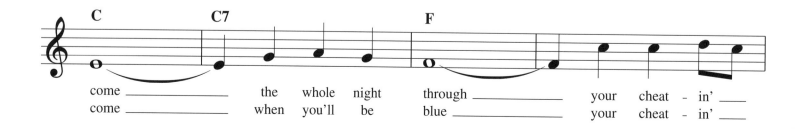

come _____ the whole night through _____ your cheat - in' ____
come _____ when you'll be blue _____ your cheat - in' ____

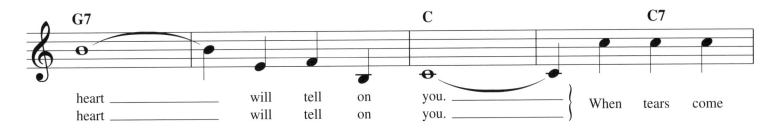

heart _____ will tell on you. _____ } When tears come
heart _____ will tell on you. _____

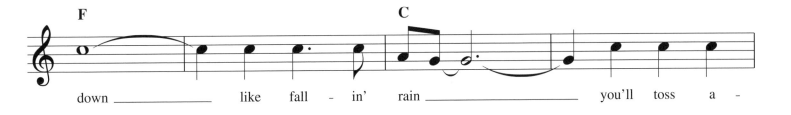

down _____ like fall - in' rain _____ you'll toss a -

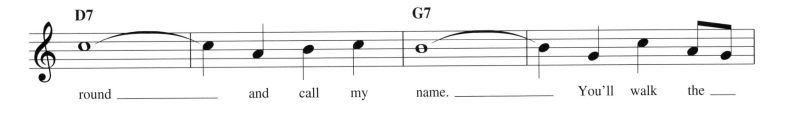

round _____ and call my name. _____ You'll walk the ___

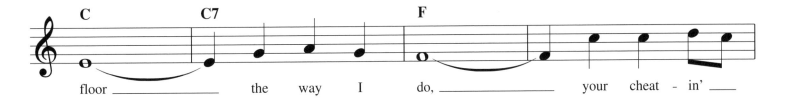

floor _____ the way I do, _____ your cheat - in' ___

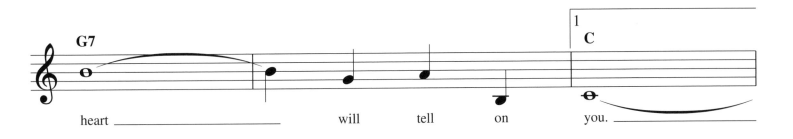

heart _____ will tell on you. _____

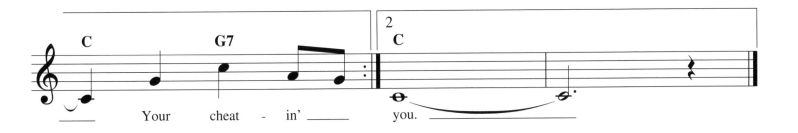

___ Your cheat - in' ___ you. _____

YOU'VE GOT A FRIEND

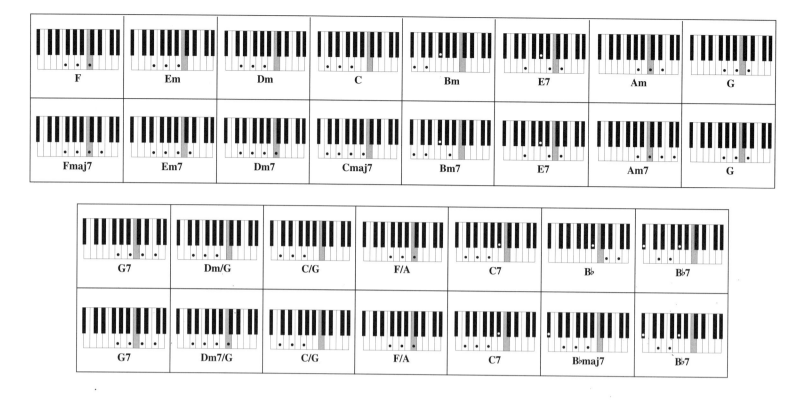

© 1971 (Renewed 1999) COLGEMS-EMI MUSIC INC.
All Rights Reserved   International Copyright Secured   Used by Permission

Words and Music by
CAROLE KING

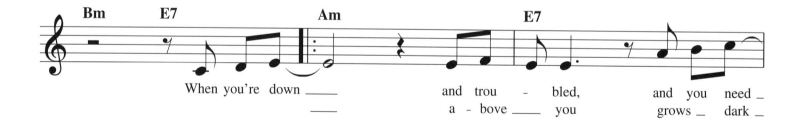

When you're down _____ and trou - bled, and you need _
_____ a - bove _____ you grows _ dark _

_____ some love and care; _____ and noth -in' _____ noth -in' is go - in' right, _
_____ and full of clouds, __ and that ol' _____ north wind be -gins _ to blow, _

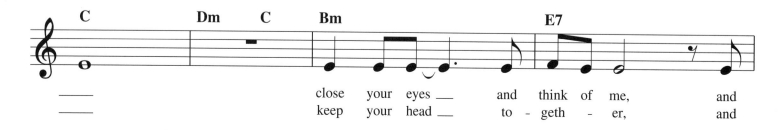

close your eyes _____ and think of me, and
keep your head _____ to - geth - er, and